# Career Flow
## A Hope-Centered Approach to Career Development

# Career Flow

## A Hope-Centered Approach to Career Development

Spencer G. Niles
*Pennsylvania State University*

Norman E. Amundson
*University of British Columbia*

Roberta A. Neault
*Life Strategies Ltd.*

Boston   Columbus   Indianapolis   New York   San Francisco   Upper Saddle River
Amsterdam   Cape Town   Dubai   London   Madrid   Milan   Munich   Paris   Montreal   Toronto
Delhi   Mexico City   Sao Paulo   Sydney   Hong Kong   Seoul   Singapore   Taipei   Tokyo

Editor-in-Chief: Jodi McPherson
Executive Editor: Sande Johnson
Development Editor: Jennifer Gessner
Editorial Assistant: Clara Ciminelli
Vice President, Director of Marketing: Margaret Waples
Executive Marketing Manager: Amy Judd
Production Editor: Annette Joseph
Editorial Production Service: Elm Street Publishing Services
Manufacturing Buyer: Megan Cochran
Electronic Composition: Integra Software Services Pvt. Ltd.
Interior Design: Elm Street Publishing Services
Photo Researchers: Annie Pickert and Jennifer Gessner
Cover Designer: Elena Sidorova

For pages 42–43: Amundson, et al., ESSENTIAL ELEMENTS OF CAREER COUNSELING, pp. 12–13, © 2009. Reproduced by permission of Pearson Education, Inc.

Library of Congress Cataloging-in-Publication Data

Niles, Spencer G.
    Career flow: a hope-centered approach to career development/Spencer G. Niles,
      Norman E. Amundson, Roberta A. Neault.—1st ed.
      p. cm.
    ISBN 978-0-13-224190-8
    1. Career development.   I. Amundson, Norman E.   II. Neault, Roberta A.   III. Title.
    HF5381.N548 2011
650.1—dc22                                      2010025842

10 9 8 7 6 5 4 3 2     EB    14 13

www.pearsonhighered.com

ISBN-10:   0-13-224190-0
ISBN-13: 978-0-13-224190-8

# Dedication

Material for this book emerged from many interactions with colleagues at Penn State University and the University of British Columbia. It is dedicated to clients and students from around the world from whom we have each learned much and have had the privilege to serve. We are each deeply grateful to our family members who have supported us throughout the development of this book. Finally, we express our gratitude to Sande Johnson and Jenny Gessner for their patience and collaboration.

S.G.N.

N.E.A.

R.A.N.

# About the Authors

**Spencer G. Niles**

Dr. Spencer Niles is Professor and Department Head for Counselor Education, Counseling Psychology, and Rehabilitation Services at Pennsylvania State University. He is the recipient of the National Career Development Association's (NCDA) Eminent Career Award, a NCDA Fellow, an American Counseling Association (ACA) Fellow, recipient of ACA's David Brooks Distinguished Mentor Award, recipient of the ACA Extended Research Award, and recipient of the University of British Columbia Noted Scholar Award. He served as president of the NCDA and editor of *The Career Development Quarterly*. Currently, he is editor of the *Journal of Counseling & Development* and has authored or co-authored approximately 100 publications and delivered more than 100 presentations on career development theory and practice. He is an Honorary Member of the Japanese Career Development Association, Honorary Member of the Italian Association for Educational and Vocational Guidance, and a Lifetime Honorary Member of the Ohio Career Development Association.

**Norman E. Amundson**

Dr. Norman Amundson is a Professor in Counseling Psychology and a member of the Faculty of Education at the University of British Columbia, Canada. He has given numerous workshops and seminars and also has been a keynote speaker at many national and international conferences. In his writings Dr. Amundson emphasizes the importance of creativity, imagination, cultural awareness, and action. His publications include *Active Engagement* (Past Winner of the Canadian Counseling Association Best Book Award), the *Essential Elements of Career Counseling*, the *Physics of Living*, and several career workbooks including *Career Pathways, Career Crossroads, Guiding Circles*, and *Career Scope*.

Dr. Amundson has won a number of academic and professional awards. Some of his recent accomplishments include: Best Research Article in the *Career Development Quarterly*–National Career Development Association; the Judy Geoghegan-Doi Distinguished Professional Service Award–National Employment Counseling Association; Honorary Lifetime Board Member of BCCDA Honorary Lifetime Member of the Swedish Career Development Association; and an Honorary Doctorate from the University of Umea, Sweden.

**Roberta A. Neault**

Dr. Roberta Neault is President of Life Strategies Ltd. and a counselor-educator at Athabasca, Yorkville, and Trinity Western universities in Canada. An oft-invited workshop facilitator, conference presenter, and keynote speaker, Dr. Neault is internationally recognized for her work in career development. Dr. Neault received the prestigious Stu Conger Award for Leadership in Career Counselling and Career Development in Canada and led a team that received the BC Career Development Award of Excellence. Her publications include *Career Strategies for a Lifetime of Success, Beyond the Basics: Real World Skills for Career Practitioners*, and *Personality Dimensions® Train-the-Trainer Toolkit,* and she is co-author of seven Personality Dimensions® topical *Toolkits for Trainers*.

# Brief Contents

# Detailed Contents

## Section III   *Visioning, Goal Setting, and Planning*

# Section IV   *Implementing*

## Section V   *Adapting*

# Features of *Career Flow*

The Career Flow metaphor lends itself to a comprehensive and realistic picture of the career experience. Experiences are rated as whitewater (high demand times), stillwater (low demand times), and optimal (an engaging and stimulating challenge level) career flow moments.

- Each moment requires specific skills to manage their respective challenges effectively.

*Essential competencies addressed*—hope, self-reflection, self-clarity, visioning, goal setting and planning, implementing and adapting—are described in detail.

- Activities are provided to help students develop these competencies for successful career self-management.

*Chapter Case Studies*—Located at the beginning of each chapter, these case studies address the respective aspects of career flow.

- Students can use the case studies to apply the concepts taught in each chapter.

*Chapter Activities*—Throughout each chapter, activities empower students to master the various aspects of their career flow.

- Students apply the concepts taught in each chapter to their own lives.

*Reflection questions and discussion tips*—Tips are infused throughout each chapter and questions for reflection/discussion are found at the end of the chapters to encourage students to consider how the concepts taught relate to their own lives.

- Promotes deeper and reflective learning.

*Additional Resources*—At the end of each chapter, students will find additional resources allowing greater understanding of their career flow.

- To expand student learning related to the various aspects of their career flow.

## A Hope-Centered Model of Career Development

Hope is at the center of:

Self-Reflection
Self-Clarity
Visioning
Goal Setting & Planning
Implementing & Adapting

# Preface

This book helps you identify essential self-characteristics—your skills, passions, personality style, and values—for making effective educational and career plans. The book also introduces you to a new way of thinking about your career. Specifically, the "career flow" metaphor is used to describe the various dimensions of the career experience all workers encounter in their jobs. For example, everyone's career includes times of great challenge, times of low demand, and times when the work demands are just right. The career flow model in this book equips you to address all of these career experiences successfully.

A cornerstone of the book is the "Hope-Centered Model of Career Development." This model emphasizes the importance of self-reflection, self-clarity, visioning, goal setting/planning, and implementing/adapting in career planning. You are introduced to each of these essential steps for career self-management. Central to all of these steps is the critical factor of hope. In this book, you will learn how hope drives all phases of career development. With it, you can use the steps outlined in the book to make effective career decisions. Without it, positive career direction becomes less likely. Strategies for bolstering your level of hope are shared in this book.

Hope becomes especially important as people engage in job searching. The book's authors explain the key strategies for successful job searching. You will learn about writing winning resumes, engaging in powerful interviews that make positive impressions, creating a network that connects you to opportunities you desire, and tapping into support networks that help you persist in the career development process.

One of the goals for this book is to provide you with a career development resource that is creative, useful, and realistic. Another goal is to help you to understand the wide range of challenges all workers encounter. Third, the book provides you with a framework for managing all aspects of your career. The authors hope you will achieve all of these goals—and more—as your career flow journey unfolds!

## Instructor Resources

*Online Instructor's Manual*   This manual is intended to give professors a framework or blueprint of ideas and suggestions that may assist them in providing their students with activities, journal writing, thought-provoking situations, and group activities. The test bank organized by chapter includes: multiple choice, true/false and short-answer questions that support the key features in the book. This supplement is available for download from the Instructor's Resource Center at http://www.pearsonhighered.com/irc

*Online PowerPoint Presentation*   A comprehensive set of PowerPoint slides that can be used by instructors for class presentations or by students for lecture preview or review. The presentation includes all the graphs and tables in the textbook. The presentation contains bullet point PowerPoint slides for each chapter. These slides highlight the important points of each chapter to help students understand the concepts within each chapter. Instructors may download these PowerPoint presentations from the Instructor's Resource Center at http://www.pearsonhighered.com/irc

*MyTest*   Pearson MyTest offers instructors a secure online environment and quality assessments to easily create print exams, study guide questions, and quizzes from any computer with an Internet connection.

*Premium Assessment Content*
- Draw from a rich library of question testbanks that complement the Pearson textbook and the course's learning objectives.
- Edit questions or tests to fit all specific teaching needs.

*Instructor Friendly Features*
- Easily create and store personalized questions, including images, diagrams, and charts using simple drag-and-drop and Word-like controls.
- Use additional information provided by Pearson, such as the question's difficulty level or learning objective, to help quickly build each test.

*Time-Saving Enhancements*
- Add headers or footers and easily scramble questions and answer choices all from one simple toolbar.
- Quickly create multiple versions of each test or answer key, and when ready, simply save to Word or PDF format and print!
- Export your exams for import to Blackboard 6.0, CE (WebCT), or Vista (WebCT)!

Additional information available at http://www.pearsonmytest.com

**mystudentsuccesslab**   Are you teaching online, in a hybrid setting, or looking to infuse exciting technology into your classroom for the first time? Then be sure to refer to the MyStudentSuccessLab section included in the coming pages of this Preface to learn more. This online solution is designed to help students build the skills they need to succeed at http://www.mystudentsuccesslab.com

## Other Resources

*"Easy access to online, book-specific Teaching support is now just a click away!"*

*Instructor Resource Center*   Register. Redeem. Login. Three easy steps that open the door to a variety of print and media resources in downloadable, digital format, available to instructors exclusively through the Pearson/Prentice Hall 'IRC'. http://www.pearsonhighered.com/irc

*"Choose from a wide range of Video resources for the classroom!"*

*Prentice Hall Reference Library: Life Skills Pack* (ISBN: 0-13-127079-6)
Contains all 4 videos, or they may be requested individually as follows:

- Learning Styles and Self-Awareness, 0-13-028502-1
- Critical and Creative Thinking, 0-13-028504-8

- Relating to Others, 0-13-028511-0
- Personal Wellness, 0-13-028514-5

*Prentice Hall Reference Library: Study Skills Pack*   (ISBN: 0-13-127080-X)
Contains all 6 videos, or they may be requested individually as follows:

- Reading Effectively, 0-13-028505-6
- Listening and Memory, 0-13-028506-4
- Note Taking and Research, 0-13-028508-0
- Writing Effectively, 0-13-028509-9
- Effective Test Taking, 0-13-028500-5
- Goal Setting and Time Management, 0-13-028503-X

*Prentice Hall Reference Library: Career Skills Pack*   (ISBN: 0-13-118529-2)
Contains all 3 videos, or they may be requested individually as follows:

- Skills for the 21st Century—Technology, 0-13-028512-9
- Skills for the 21st Century—Math and Science, 0-13-028513-7
- Managing Career and Money, 0-13-028516-1

*Complete Reference Library—Life/Study Skills/Career Video Pack on DVD*
(ISBN: 0-13-501095-0)

- Our Reference Library of thirteen popular video resources has now been digitized onto one DVD so students and instructors alike can benefit from the array of video clips. Featuring Life Skills, Study Skills, and Career Skills, they help to reinforce the course content in a more interactive way.

*Faculty Video Resources*

- Teacher Training Video 1: Critical Thinking, ISBN: 0-13-099432-4
- Teacher Training Video 2: Stress Management & Communication, ISBN: 0-13-099578-9
- Teacher Training Video 3: Classroom Tips, ISBN: 0-13-917205-X
- Student Advice Video, ISBN: 0-13-233206-X
- Study Skills Video, ISBN: 0-13-096095-0

*Current Issues Videos*

- ABC News Video Series: Student Success Second Edition, ISBN: 0-13-031901-5
- ABC News Video Series: Student Success Third Edition, ISBN: 0-13-152865-3

*MyStudentSuccessLab PH Videos on DVD*   (ISBN: 0-13-514249-0)

- Our six most popular video resources have been digitized onto one DVD so students and instructors alike can benefit from the array of video clips. Featuring Technology, Math and Science, Managing Money and Career, Learning Styles and Self-Awareness, Study Skills, and Peer Advice, they help to reinforce the course content in a more interactive way. They are also accessible through our MSSL and course management offerings and available on VHS.

*"Through partnership opportunities, we offer a variety of Assessment options!"*

*LASSI*  The LASSI is a 10-scale, 80-item assessment of students' awareness about and use of learning and study strategies. Addressing skill, will and self-regulation, the focus is on both covert and overt thoughts, behaviors, attitudes and beliefs that relate to successful learning and that can be altered through educational interventions. Available in two formats: Paper ISBN: 0-13-172315-4 or Online ISBN: 0-13-172316-2 (access card).

*Noel Levitz/RMS*  This retention tool measures Academic Motivation, General Coping Ability, Receptivity to Support Services, PLUS Social Motivation. It helps identify at-risk students, the areas with which they struggle, and their receptiveness to support. Available in paper or online formats, as well as short and long versions. Paper Long Form A: ISBN: 0-13-512066-7; Paper Short Form B: ISBN: 0-13-512065-9; Online Forms A,B & C: ISBN: 0-13-098158-3.

*Robbins Self Assessment Library*  This compilation teaches students to create a portfolio of skills. S.A.L. is a self-contained, interactive library of 49 behavioral questionnaires that help students discover new ideas about themselves, their attitudes, and their personal strengths and weaknesses. Available in Paper, CD-Rom, and Online (Access Card) formats.

*Readiness for Education at a Distance Indicator (READI)*  READI is a web-based tool that assesses the overall likelihood for online learning success. READI generates an immediate score and a diagnostic interpretation of results, including recommendations for successful participation in online courses and potential remediation sources. Please visit www.readi.info for additional information. ISBN: 0-13-188967-2.

*Pathway to Student Success CD-ROM*  The CD is divided into several categories, each of which focuses on a specific topic that relates to students and provides them with the context, tools and strategies to enhance their educational experience. ISBN: 0-13-239314-X.

*The Golden Personality Type Profiler*  The Golden Personality Type Profiler™ helps students understand how they make decisions and relate to others. By completing the Golden Personality Type Profiler™ students develop a deeper understanding of their strengths, a clearer picture of how their behavior impacts others, and a better appreciation for the interpersonal style of others and how to interact with them more effectively. Using these results as a guide, students will gain the self awareness that is key to professional development and success. ISBN: 0-13-706654-6.

*"For a truly tailored solution that fosters campus connections and increases retention, talk with us about Custom publishing."*

*Pearson Custom Publishing*  We are the largest custom provider for print and media shaped to your course's needs. Please visit us at http://www.pearson custom.com to learn more.

# Student Support

Tools to help make the grade now, and excel in school later.

*"Today's students are more inclined than ever to use Technology to enhance their learning."*

mystudentsuccesslab    Refer to the **MyStudentSuccessLab** section of this Preface to learn about our revolutionary resource (http://www.mystudentsuccesslab.com). This online solution is designed to help students build the skills they need to succeed.

*"Time management is the #1 challenge students face." We can help.*

*Prentice Hall Planner*    A basic planner that includes a monthly & daily calendar plus other materials to facilitate organization. 8.5x11.

*Premier Annual Planner*    This specially designed, annual 4-color collegiate planner includes an academic planning/resources section, monthly planning section (2 pages/month), weekly planning section (48 weeks; July start date), which facilitate short-term as well as long-term planning.  Spiral bound, 6x9. Customization is available.

*"Journaling activities promote self-discovery and self-awareness."*

*Student Reflection Journal*    Through this vehicle, students are encouraged to track their progress and share their insights, thoughts, and concerns. $8^{1}/_{2}$ x 11. 90 pages.

*"The Student Orientation Series includes short booklets on specialized topics that facilitate greater student understanding."*

*S.O.S. Guides*    These help students understand what these opportunities are, how to take advantage of them, and how to learn from their peers while doing so. They include:

- Connolly: *Learning Communities*, ISBN: 0-13-232243-9
- Hoffman: *Stop Procrastination Now! 10 Simple and SUCCESSFUL Steps for Student Success*, ISBN: 0-13-513056-5
- Jabr: *English Language Learners*, ISBN: 0-13-232242-0
- Watts: *Service Learning*, ISBN: 0-13-232201-0

# Acknowledgments

The authors are grateful to our clients who have taught us so much about the career development experience. We also thank our students who have provided the testing ground for the ideas we have included in this book. Numerous workshop participants around the world also provided feedback regarding the career flow model. Hyung Joon Yoon helped create the hope-centered figure and self-assessment used in the book, and Fiona Glendinning provided important input and feedback to earlier versions of the book. Our family members also were a constant source of support to us throughout this project.

We are also very grateful to our editing team, Sande Johnson and Jenny Gessner from Merrill Prentice Hall, who worked with us each step of the way, encouraging us to keep focused on the goals for the book. They believed in our project—and in us. We thank them, along with our reviewers: Tim Buecher, University of Southern Indiana; Gwendolyne Eileen Bunch, Columbia College; Bruce Cottew, Sullivan University; Debra L. Hartman, DeVry University; Marilyn Joseph, Everest College; Tina Mello, Northeastern University; Connie Pilato, Jamestown Community College; Stephen Strachman, Hudson Valley Community College; Edward M. Tucker, Lincoln College of Technology; Marvin Turk, College of the Sequoias; Kathy Wenell-Nesbit, Chippewa Valley Technical College; Marilyn C. Wilson, Massachusetts Institute of Technology.

# PEARSON
# mystudentsuccesslab™

**Succeed in college and beyond!**
**Connect, practice, and personalize with MyStudentSuccessLab.**

**www.mystudentsuccesslab.com**

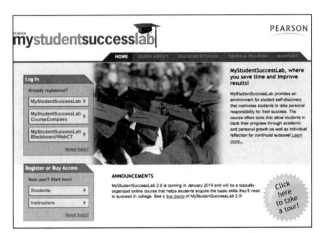

**MyStudentSuccessLab** is an online solution designed to help students acquire the skills they need to succeed. They will have access to peer-led video presentations and develop core skills through interactive exercises and projects that provide academic, life, and career skills that will transfer to ANY course.

**It can accompany any Student Success text, or be sold as a stand-alone course offering.** Often students try to learn material without applying the information. To become a successful learner, they must consistently apply techniques to their daily activities.

## MyStudentSuccessLab provides students with opportunities to become successful learners:

**Connect:**
• Engage with real students through video interviews on key issues.

**Practice:**
• Three skill-building exercises per topic provide interactive experience and practice.

**Personalize:**
• Apply what is learned to your life.
• Create a personal project that will be graded and can be posted to your portfolio.
• Journal online and set short- and long-term goals.

**Resources**
• Tools to use: Plagiarism Guide, Dictionary, Calculators, and a Multimedia index of Interative case and activities.

**Text-Specific Study Plan**
• Chapter Objectives provide clear expectations.
• Practice Tests for each chapter of your text assess your current understanding.
 • Completion of each practice test generates a study plan that is unique to you.
• Enrichment activities identify strengths and weaknesses, provide immediate feedback, and link to additional media.
• Flashcards help you study and review.

**Assessments**
• Includes Career Assessment tool, Learning Styles, and Personality Styles.

# PEARSON
# mystudentsuccesslab™

## Succeed in college and beyond!
## Connect, practice, and personalize with MyStudentSuccessLab.

### www.mystudentsuccesslab.com

**MyStudentSuccessLab** is an online solution designed to help instructors engage their students in the course content, provide practice on skill development, and assess mastery. Additional resources, including sample syllabi, guide, assigments, and rubrics are included.

### MyStudentSuccessLab saves class prep time and supports implementation:
### Instructor Tool/Support:

• **Sample syllabus**—provided to ensure easy implementation.

• **Instructor's guide**—includes information that describes each activity, the skills each addresses, an estimated student time on task for each exercise, and a granding rubric for the final Apply activity.

• **Additional Assignments**—Extra suggested activities to use with each topic:

1. General activity related to an important objective for each topic.
2. Internet use Assignment (e.g. Google "YouTube" video on topic) to find a video on key strategies and write a critique and present it to the class.
3. Student Resource tool usage (e.g. Read and take online notes on the main points of the Understanding Plagiarism guide).

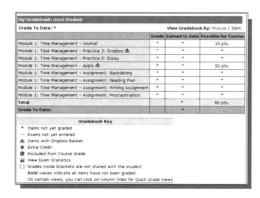

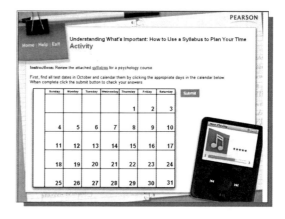

### MyStudentSuccessLab is easy to use and assign.
### Support is available in the following ways:

• Visit **www.mystudentsuccesslab.com** under "Tours and Training" and "Support."
• Contact your local sales professional.
• Send an inquiry to **Student.Success@pearson.com** for additional support.
• Join one of our weekly WebEx traning sessions.
• Request on-campus training with a Faculty Advocate for qualified adoptions.
• Access technical support 24 hours a day, seven days a week, at **http://247pearsoned.custhelp.com**.

"We all have possibilities we don't know about. We can do things we don't even dream we can do. "

—Dale Carnegie

# Introducing Career Flow

## OBJECTIVES

This chapter focuses on the career flow metaphor. After reading this chapter, you will be able to:

- Describe the career flow metaphor
- Understand the relationship between career flow and self-awareness
- Understand the importance of career flow

## CASE STUDY

Alice met with her career counselor at State University to discuss her recently completed summer work experience. She had worked with an accounting firm as an intern between her junior and senior years of college. She was concerned that she found her workdays fun, boring, challenging, fast-paced, and more. Entering her first work experience related to her academic major, she expected to find each day to be enjoyable and meaningful. Alice was thrown by the variability in her experience. Although there were many positive moments, there were also moments that were anything but positive. Is this how it was supposed to be? Did her negative experiences mean she had chosen the wrong career and/or the wrong academic major? She felt panic as she considered these questions while walking to the career center for her appointment. She hoped her career counselor would be able to reassure her, but she wasn't sure what to expect.

Alice's first work experience related to her academic major was a bit of a "shocker." It was good, bad, positive, and negative. She was excited to enter the internship and looked forward to her work. What she had not planned for were the challenges she encountered. Alice was having trouble integrating these experiences into her overall understanding of what a work experience should be like. In essence, she had expected her experience to flow much more smoothly. The "rough waters" she encountered in her internship and their implications for her future plans shook her. Were they dire signs of a poor career choice? Were they indications of issues she needed to address in order to become a better prospective employee? What should she think at this point, and what should she do?

The answers to these questions, to a great degree, depend on how you conceptualize career development. Often, people think about work the same way they think about—and sometimes question—relationships. Specifically, a person might wonder if difficult times could mean a poor choice in a partner or, in Alice's instance, a career. Although this can be true, it would be unrealistic to expect one's work (and one's relationships) to always be blissful and positive. In all careers, there are challenges and rewards. Sometimes, things go smoothly—perhaps even effortlessly. There are other times, however, when it feels like a constant uphill struggle. There are times of excitement and times of boredom. Thus, in managing your career effectively, it is important to be able to handle the positive as well as the challenging aspects of your work. To be sure, there are times when changing a job (or a partner) may make the most sense but, many times, navigating your career experiences effectively depends on having a realistic understanding of work, a confident and positive attitude, and the requisite skills to handle what comes your way.

## The Career Flow Metaphor

The career flow metaphor was developed during a bike ride along the banks of the Fraser River in British Columbia, Canada. Observing the many currents of the river led to the notion that these currents seemed similar to the many dimensions of the work experience. Although that statement may seem a bit unusual at first, take a moment to think about it. A river has rapids, still waters, eddies, steady currents, twists, and bends. Depending on the currents, navigating them can be easy, challenging, overwhelming, or boring. In a similar way, your career will have moments when work demands will be overwhelming; moments when the work demands will be minimal; and moments when your work tasks will occur at a steady and manageable rate. There will be unexpected challenges and predictable moments. You will encounter tasks for which you will feel well prepared and those for which you feel totally unprepared. Each dimension of your work experience will require you to respond

*It is important to adapt to changes.*

istockphoto

in specific ways to manage your career effectively. Having a realistic attitude toward work and possessing the requisite skills for handling the challenges you will undoubtedly experience will help you to be a positive employee and to experience maximal work satisfaction. In other words, your attitude and skills will go a long way in determining the outcome of your work behavior; that is, whether you are successful. Because work experiences vary in ways that resemble how a river flows, we have chosen to use the term *career flow* to help you acquire a full understanding of the career experience.

Before offering further explanation regarding this term, we invite you to consider what comes to mind when you hear the term *career flow*. Take a moment right now to write down anything you think of related to this term.

Each time this question has been posed, a wide range of responses emerges. Here are some of those responses:

| | |
|---|---|
| Serendipitous | Floating |
| Rate of travel | Passive |
| Continuous | Movement |
| Flexibility | Happiness |
| Danger | Energizing |
| Positive growth | Organic |
| Compelling | Directional |
| Goal-focused | Consuming |
| Going with the flow | Natural |
| Sense of ease | |

Interestingly, these words describe positive experiences—for example, positive growth, energizing, uplifting—as well as what many might view as less than positive experiences—lack of control, danger. So which is correct? Does the term *career flow* depict a positive energizing experience or does it involve dangerous experiences over which one has little control? Based on what you have read thus far, you likely have surmised that it is both.

With each different experience of the river, you had to use certain strategies and skills to navigate that particular part of the river successfully. For example, in whitewater, strong paddling skills and knowledge of river currents were required to navigate the rapids. In still water, you needed to generate momentum using your power and strength to move along the river. When the challenges of the river matched your skill

*Focused activity using your skills while working on things you enjoy places you "in the flow."*

Shutterstock

*Career Flow Imagination*

ACTIVITY 1.1    Imagine you are paddling a canoe down a river. As you move along, note your areas of comfort versus stress and enjoyment versus boredom. Notice what the experience is like as you paddle through slow, still water. Now imagine the currents shifting to an extended "whitewater" experience as the current reaches maximum speed. Consider the varying levels of effort and the different skills required to paddle your canoe at various places on the river. As the currents change, so too do the skills and effort required. Do you have a preference for one type of current over the others?

_____

What did you like about each part of the river?

_____

What did you not like about each part of the river?

_____

level, then it was likely that you experienced a positive journey as you moved through the water. When the challenges exceeded your resources, you may have felt overwhelmed and discouraged. When your resources surpassed the challenges, then you may have felt bored and stagnant.

There are similarities between how you must navigate different aspects of how the river flows and the challenges you encounter in your career journey. At all times in your career, specific strengths and characteristics become essential for managing how your career flows. Developing these strengths increases your ability to manage your career flow in a way you find satisfying.

Too often, people approach their careers with unrealistic expectations; that is, they seem to be searching for the ultimate occupational opportunity that brings with it constant satisfaction, meaning, and purpose. Alice certainly brought this expectation with her into her internship. Although that expectation is clearly desirable, you may be setting yourself up for failure if you expect your work experience to be characterized primarily by such positive conditions. Alice was thrown by these realities. Her less than ideal experiences caused her to question her occupational choice. She was applying unrealistic expectations to her work experience. In this sense, there really are no occupational nirvanas—all work experiences have their joys and their challenges.

However, there are occupations that provide many hours of satisfying work in which you use the skills you value as you engage in activities you find interesting. Likewise, there are occupations that will provide you with the opportunity to interact with people who possess similar values and interests. Occupations that will add to the sense of meaning and purpose you find in your life can also be found.

Undoubtedly, even in these very positive situations, however, you will also experience challenges. On some days, things will not go as you prefer, coworkers

*Shutterstock*

*Do what you enjoy and find others with similar interests.*

will seem a source of unbearable agitation, and you may be knee-deep in tasks that are uninspiring at best and deadly boring at worst. Thus, the goal is not to construct a career in which such experiences do not exist but rather to seek opportunities in which such experiences are the exception rather than the rule. Moreover, it is important to develop the essential skills for coping with the challenging times as effectively as possible. Developing these skills empowers you to identify what you need to do to manage any situation you encounter in your career development.

Tip    *There is something to learn from every experience.*

Managing your career development effectively requires a substantial amount of career- and self-awareness. This is particularly true when you encounter challenges in your career. The career flow metaphor is designed to help you think in new ways about challenges you encounter and the strategies you can use to manage those challenges. This is especially true with challenges you have struggled with for an extended period of time (for many, making an occupational choice is one of those challenges). It is easy in these situations to begin to feel hopeless and maybe even helpless. You can begin to feel there is no clear solution to your challenge. For example, perhaps you have struggled for some time to identify a college major you feel excited about. Perhaps you have even selected a major only to find later that it was not what you thought it was and you were left feeling confused and unsure once again. Perhaps, a bit like Alice, you felt stuck in your career development. If you currently are in a situation similar to this, then the career flow metaphor may help you to think systematically about your career journey.

It is important not to confuse career flow with *flow*, a term used in psychology that refers to peak or optimal experiences in living. In this book, the term *career flow* is used in a much broader sense, representing the total work experience—both positive and negative. Each dimension of career flow plays an important part in shaping your life; however, the contribution of the different facets of career flow often is not recognized. For instance, when overwhelmed by the demands of work, we often are unable to appreciate the lessons to be learned in such moments. Other times, we may wonder where the challenge is and feel as if "the thrill is gone" from our daily work activities and interpret our work experiences as meaningless. Still other times, we may feel as though everything we do requires substantial effort—a sense of accomplishment seems an elusive goal never meant to be achieved—and so we become discouraged.

Each of these experiences is a crucial aspect of career development. They provide environmental feedback regarding ways you may need to change your course, stay the course, or do a little of both. They can be indicators that help you pay attention to your experiences and respond accordingly. Unfortunately, we often ignore information provided to us, sometimes out of fear of what it might mean. For example, you could imagine that one poor test grade in an academic major or one negative work experience in which you do not perform adequately means you have made a serious mistake in choosing a particular career goal. Rather, it could simply mean you have identified an area for increased effort aimed at developing a reasonable level of competence in one aspect of your career goal. We sometimes ignore this possibility because we fear we might not be up to the challenge. Other times, the evidence may be overwhelming that a significant change of course is needed, but we often equate changing with failing and attempt to deny reality.

When we fail to pay close attention to the variety of experiences comprising our career flow, we miss opportunities to construct careers that bring a more complete sense of meaning and purpose. Thus, one of the most important skills in managing your career flow is simply paying attention. As famously declared in the play, *Death of a Salesman*: "Attention must be paid"—so it is, with your career. Paying attention to your experience and the feedback you get regarding your career plans will provide a useful guide in constructing future goals.

## Career Flow and Self-Awareness

To create a career that flows in a satisfying way, you must pay attention to the daily "noise" you encounter and create. In this context, noise refers to the inner dialog you engage in over the course of a day. What do you tell yourself? What do you think about your situation? Becoming aware of your "self-talk" helps you gain greater self-awareness. Once you become aware of your self-talk, you will be able to identify

### *Self-Thoughts Journal*

ACTIVITY 1.2        To gain clarity in your inner conversations, start maintaining a daily journal. Try to record at least a few thoughts each day. Begin right now by recording a few words for each of these questions:

- In what ways do you encourage yourself?

- In what ways do you discourage yourself?

_____

- What positive statements do you make about yourself?

_____

- Conversely, what negative statements do you tell yourself?

_____

- In what ways do you feel you do not measure up?

_____

- What are your strengths?

_____

- What would someone who loves you say are your strengths?

_____

- Where do you find enjoyment in your activities?

_____

- What sort of activities do you prefer to avoid?

_____

- What do you hope for in your life?

_____

- What do you fear?

_____

This task should only take a few minutes. Write down (or type) whatever comes to mind as you consider these questions. Do not judge what you record; just go with what comes to mind.

ways in which your thoughts are helpful to you and ways in which they are not helpful. The thoughts that are not helpful can be challenged, changed, and discontinued.

Now, look back over what you have written. Does anything surprise you? No doubt many things you wrote are familiar to you. Try to look at what you have written in an objective way. What makes sense to you and what does not? What is your rationale for each? Are there things you would like to change about what you wrote? Are there things you would like to develop further? What seems to be stopping you in both cases? Do you see a negative pattern you can change? For example, you may choose to decrease the amount of time you spend thinking about the faults of others or you may choose to spend less time being critical of yourself. Similarly, is there one thing you would like to do more of? You may choose to say nicer things to yourself more often during the day, for example. Try one of these out over the course of the next couple of days and see how it goes. Do not judge the results as good or bad, but rather be like a scientist—consider the different behaviors and/or ways of thinking as if they were an experiment. See how the experiment goes, and then assess how you feel (better, worse, hopeful, discouraged, etc.). Once you have tried this experiment, you may find it useful to discuss your thoughts about it with a career counselor.

Continue recording your responses to these questions (adding your own) on a daily basis for the next couple of months. Over the course of just a few weeks, you will begin to notice patterns. You will be able to see the ways in which you maintain a positive outlook and the ways in which you tend to be more negative. You will see what your preoccupations are and what your fears may be. In fact, your preoccupations have much to suggest relative to what occupations you may choose to enter.

On the other hand, fearful thoughts can limit your capacity to imagine the possibilities. Once you become aware of your limiting thoughts, you can begin to examine them more closely. You can challenge the accuracy of negative beliefs and judging self-statements. As you challenge these, try to stay mindful of the fact that no one is perfect—everyone makes mistakes and judgment errors. What is important, then, is learning from these mistakes and giving yourself permission to be less than perfect.

You can also begin to pay closer attention to your hopes and the positive elements in your life. It is essential that you acknowledge these—underline them, highlight them in bright colors, and begin to consider ways to build on them. Look for opportunities to engage more frequently in positive thoughts and behaviors. One way to do this is developing a social network of like-minded people; that is, those who enjoy and value similar positive activities as you. Building on the positive elements in your life will help you to experience greater joy and happiness in your life.

Tip    *All effective career decisions are grounded in self-awareness.*

## The Importance of Career Flow

The different dimensions of career flow shape the course of your life and help you tune in to what you enjoy and what you value. They represent a holistic sense of the human experience—excitement, boredom, confidence, anxiety, love, and hate. Everyone has these experiences, and they cannot be eliminated from your career experience. So, even though "occupational nirvanas" are nonexistent, satisfying careers do exist. One of the keys in constructing a satisfying career is to learn from the totality of your career and life experiences. Learning from all of your career experiences allows you to be more intentional and systematic in pursuing meaningful and positive career opportunities.

It is important to remember that you can learn how to respond effectively to each of the challenges your career presents to you. At times, your career will flow smoothly; at other times, you will experience excessive amounts of challenge leading to a sense of being overwhelmed with the tasks at hand. Fortunately, the ebb and flow of career development processes also include times when the demands confronting you will be minimal. Your resources far exceed the challenges you encounter. These can be times of renewal from recent activities and re-imagining future possibilities. You can develop the resources for managing each dimension of your career experience.

Developing these resources is perhaps more important today than in previous decades. Increasingly, workers around the world appear to be experiencing greater levels of work overload. A survey of U.S. workers indicates that 62 percent leave work feeling "overtired" and "overwhelmed" (Schwartz, 2003). The average worker in the United States now spends more than 1,800 hours per year at work. Increased work participation must come at the expense of participating in other life roles, many of which (e.g., leisure, family time) can serve as buffers against work-related stress. Chronic stress creates physiological and psychological changes and often leads to disease and depression.

Understanding the range of experiences comprising the career development experience will help you to manage your career more effectively. Knowing that your work will bring you challenges you prefer and challenges you would rather not experience will help you to keep a proper perspective related to your work. Developing the skills necessary for managing the various ways your career flows will help you become more satisfied in work and life.

## Summary

Everyone's career has both challenges and rewards. There are times when careers flow smoothly and times when they do not. Managing your career flow effectively begins with awareness. By first paying attention to your inner dialog, you begin to develop the awareness necessary for identifying what is occurring in your environment, how you are reacting to your experiences, and what you need to do to cope effectively with the tasks confronting you. You can develop strategies to cope effectively with the inevitable range of career flow experiences you will encounter.

## Questions for Reflection and Discussion

1. Using the career flow concept, what advice would you offer Alice relative to her current career concerns?

2. Consider what you hope to accomplish in your career. Write down three potential goals you have for your career development.

3. Be intentional about saying three positive things about yourself over the next week. Practice this once in the morning and once in the evening. Pay attention to what this experience is like for you. Consider recording your thoughts in a journal.

4. Discuss with a classmate your reactions to "career flow." In what ways does it make sense to you? In what ways does it not?

5. We recommend you read one or two biographies or autobiographies of people you admire. As you read these stories, try to identify the different dimensions of career flow experienced by the person you are reading about. How did she or he manage the different dimensions of career flow? What did this person manage well? What did he or she manage less effectively? When you finish your reading, write down three lessons you learned about career flow from your reading.

## Reference

Schwartz, N. D. (2003, November 24). Will 'Made in USA' fade away? *Fortune, 148,* 11, 98–110.

> " Believe in yourself! Have faith in your abilities! Without a humble but reasonable confidence in your own powers you cannot be successful or happy. "
>
> —*Norman Vincent Peale*

# Essential Career Flow Competencies

## OBJECTIVES

This chapter focuses on a hope-centered approach to career decision making. After reading this chapter, you will be able to:

- Understand the importance of hope in career and educational planning
- Understand the importance of self-reflection and self-clarity in educational and career planning
- Understand the difference between objective and subjective career development
- Use self-clarity to envision future possibilities

## CASE STUDY

"My dream started out as an ambition to set foot on each of the seven continents and experience the people, culture, and heartbeat of a foreign land. I began this dream by saving for a trip to Europe at age fifteen. I spent that summer living with a family in Germany, and learned to immerse myself in another world. We learn so much by stepping beyond our comfort level and challenging the mind and spirit. That first trip became a lifelong obsession that led me to Iceland, India, Russia, the Great Barrier Reef, Fiji, the Maldive and Seychelle Islands, Nepal, Vietnam, Malaysia, and the Serengeti in Africa via overland truck for eleven weeks, just to name a few.

In 1978, after graduating from an all women's college in Iowa, I began working as a special education and elementary education teacher in Colorado. My desire to impact children's lives through teaching lasted for twenty years, and still continues today. I have always maintained a strong connection with family and friends, and, in 1993, I was inspired by my father's dream to climb Mt. Kilimanjaro in Africa. This led us to a successful summit of "Kili" on my dad's 61st birthday. He was my inspiration, my friend, and my hero, and six years later another climb of one of the world's highest peaks was set in motion. With a successful millennium summit of Mt. Aconcagua, South America's highest peak, the idea to climb the "Seven Summits" was born.

My dream of climbing intensified after my diagnosis of Multiple Sclerosis in 1999. Waking up with a body that was numb, I feared the worst. I quit my twenty-year teaching career, left a twenty-two year marriage and felt the panic of needing to complete my chosen task while I was still in control of my physical body. From that point, I saved money when and where I could, and in 2000 used what I had saved to participate in a climb of Mera Peak in Nepal, to raise money for a charity. Next, I was off to Russia to climb Europe's highest peak, Mount Elbrus. With my health still strong, I trained on Mexican volcanoes for an attempt of Denali the following spring. With an investment of $10,000 in extreme weather gear, along with a determination that would not stop, I reached the summit of Denali in May of 2006.

Upon returning from Denali, I was told that my persistent back pain was caused by a cyst on a nerve in my spine, which was being pinched between two disks. The cyst developed from a slow leak of spinal fluid, due to a faulty spinal tap by a young medical student, when I was first diagnosed with MS in 1999. After back surgery in 2006, and recovery time followed by training to rebuild my strength, I am ready to move forward again. With ice axe in hand and the desire to complete my dream of setting foot on each continent and climbing the "Seven Summits," I climbed Australia's Mt. Kosciusko in July of 2008, and Mt. Vinson in Antarctica in November 2008. I saved the best for last and set foot on the top of the world, Mt. Everest, on May 23, 2009.

I have been blessed in my life with many gifts, including opportunities to travel and climb. These experiences have enriched my life, and for that I am truly grateful. My biggest reward through all of this has been learning about overcoming fear and limitations, and sharing this lesson with others. My desire to impact children's lives has extended to adults and people with disabilities as well. I now give presentations with the message of encouraging others to empower themselves. It is in giving that we receive our greatest gifts.

So my dreams go on, my hopes and health are strong, and I approach my future with a positive outlook. The one vital lesson that I have learned through all of this is not to let your limitations define you, and never let go of your dreams. Life is too short not to go for the gusto when you are given the opportunity. I hope that all of your dreams come true as well."

Lori Schneider, www.EmpowermentThroughAdventure.com. Reprinted by permission.

There are important underlying attitudes and behaviors you must develop to effectively address the various dimensions of career flow you will experience. Developing these competencies will empower you to cope successfully with the career challenges you experience now and in the future. Specifically, career flow competencies include: (1) hope, (2) self-reflection, (3) self-clarity, (4) visioning, (5) goal setting/planning, and (6) implementing/adapting. These competencies draw on the *human agency theory*, developed by well-known Stanford University psychologist Albert Bandura. Human agency relates to understanding who you are and developing, implementing, and adjusting plans based on new learning. Collectively, these competencies provide the foundation you can use to address career flow challenges. In this chapter, these competencies are discussed in detail.

## Hope in Educational and Career Planning

### Hope

Being hopeful is essential for managing the career flow experience. Hopefulness relates to envisioning a meaningful goal and believing that positive outcomes are likely to occur should you take specific actions. Having a sense of hope allows you to consider the possibilities in any situation and propels you to take action. The late Charles Snyder (a psychologist who studied hope) defined hope in this way: "the perceived capability to derive pathways to desired goals, and motivate oneself via agency thinking to use those pathways" (2002, p. 249). Hope involves being able to identify meaningful goals toward which you are motivated to strive. It also involves the capacity to develop specific strategies for achieving those goals.

Without hope, people are not likely to take positive action in their lives. In a study of graduate students, two researchers (Alexander & Onwuegbuzie, 2007) found that students with higher levels of hope were less likely to procrastinate on tasks such as writing papers, studying for tests, and completing reading assignments when compared to students with lower levels of hope. The results of this study remind us of the pervasive importance of having a sense of hope as you manage all aspects of your career development. Thus, as depicted in Figure 2.1, hope is a central competency for managing your career flow. Hope helps you believe that you will be able to take specific steps to achieve future goals.

FIGURE 2.1    **Hope/Goal Attainment Continuum**

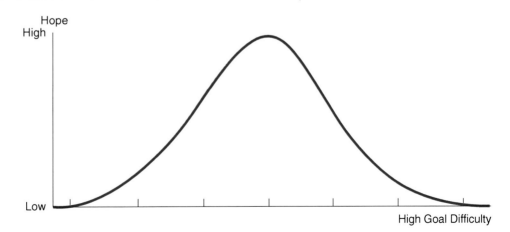

FIGURE 2.2    **The Career Flow Competencies**

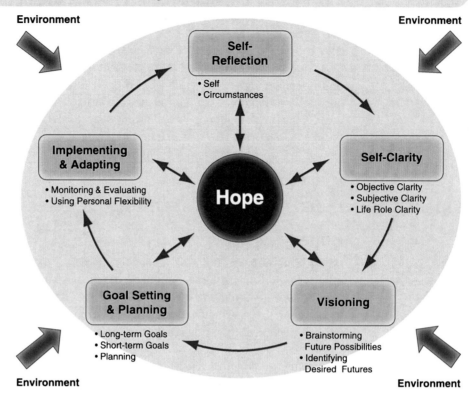

It seems obvious to state that for a person to even be willing to consider future possibilities, he or she must have a sense of hope as to what the future can entail. In discussing the relationship between hope and goal setting, Snyder (2002) contends that goals necessitating hope must fall in the middle of a probability of attainment continuum. This continuum ranges from goals you are certain you will attain to goals you believe are not possible to achieve. If the probability of attaining a goal is either 0 or 100 percent, then hope is irrelevant for such goals; therefore, goals must be meaningful and achievable but also challenging. Thus, the highest level of hope is needed for goals that offer some challenge but not too little or too much; that is, goals that fall in the middle of the difficulty continuum (see Figure 2.1 on p. 13).

Having a hopeful attitude also enables you to identify one or more action steps you can take to reach your goals. When you encounter barriers to achieving your goals, you must demonstrate *personal flexibility* to identify and pursue action steps around the obstacles that will allow you to achieve your goals. Personal flexibility involves the ability to change with change; that is, while you have specific goals identified, you are also open to new information that may influence your goals by either reinforcing them or leading you to develop new ones. Adapting to new information in this way is essential because you are constantly evolving and opportunities—both planned and unplanned—present themselves to you continually. Without hope, however, none of this is possible. You would simply give up when you encounter obstacles (and everyone encounters obstacles to their goals). Researchers have found that students low in hope tend to avoid tasks that are necessary to achieve their goals. For example, if students think they are likely to fail a test, they might delay studying for it because they have little hope that studying will lead to a successful outcome (passing the test). A good starting point for considering the importance of hope is to reread the case study provided at the beginning of this chapter and then complete the following activity.

Shutterstock

*Hope helps you persevere when the going gets tough.*

## The Case of Lori

ACTIVITY 2.1

Refer to the case example at the beginning of the chapter. This is a true story about a woman named Lori Schneider; you can view her website at: www.empowerment throughadventure.com/. Using Lori's story, respond to the following questions:

What obstacles did Lori encounter?

_____

How important was hope for Lori?

_____

How did hope help her achieve her goals?

_____

How might Lori's dream be different if she lacked hope?

_____

In what ways was Lori flexible in identifying new pathways to achieve her goal?

_____

Lori's story illustrates clearly how important hope is in envisioning a dream, setting goals, making plans, and taking actions. Lori encountered challenges to achieving her goal but hope propelled her to keep moving forward. How was she able to do this in the face of significant adversity? In identifying her goal, she first engaged in *self-reflection*, which required her to identify what was important to her (her interests), what she enjoyed (her values), and what skills she possessed and wanted to develop further. Developing answers to questions such as these resulted in *self-clarity*, which she used to engage in *visioning* as she considered future possibilities that were desirable to her. Hope empowered her to consider future possibilities and to identify a specific long-term goal that connected meaningfully to her values, interests, skills, and experiences. Her goal was indeed challenging, but not impossible.

Lori then, initially at the age of 15, made plans for achieving her goal ("to set foot on each of the seven continents and experience the people, culture, and heartbeat of a foreign land"). As she began *implementing* her plan to achieve her goal, Lori was diagnosed with multiple sclerosis. This new information certainly created an obstacle to achieving her goal. This diagnosis required her to evaluate whether her goal was still achievable, and it also required Lori to adjust her plans. Without hope, it would have been perfectly understandable if Lori had chosen at this point to give up on her dream. Yet, she did not give up. Her goal was deeply meaningful to her, so much so that she notes that upon learning her diagnosis, she intensified her commitment to her dream. In other words, her diagnosis was a choice point for her. Lori chose to continue taking actions to achieve her dream. No doubt, her diagnosis resulted in Lori adjusting her plans (personal flexibility) as she adapted to her new circumstances. This process propelled her to engage in further self-reflection resulting in self-clarity as a person with a serious physical challenge, but she continued to follow her dream and she adjusted her plans to achieve her goal. Hope was the fuel that propelled her into action.

Lori's story highlights how you can use each of the career flow competencies to manage your career flow. In essence, Lori's story underscores the importance of using hope to engage in self-reflection to develop self-clarity. Her hope provides the foundation for future possibilities she envisions and helps her to identify a meaningful goal. Because she is hopeful and has a goal, she is able to make specific plans to achieve her goal. She then implements plans of action directed toward achieving her goal while remaining open to revising her plans as they interact with her circumstances. As Lori implements her plans, she will learn more about herself and the world as a result of the actions she has taken. It is, in fact, a never-ending process. The key is paying attention to what you learn about yourself and using this new learning to inform your future course of action.

## How Hopeful Are You?

ACTIVITY 2.2          Consider the following questions:

- Are you hopeful as you consider your future? Use a scale of 1 (not hopeful) to 5 (extremely hopeful) and rate your level of hope.

- Identify what stops you from being hopeful. Write down a list of factors that limit your hope.

- Now, consider what steps you could take to increase your level of hope. Identify two steps you can take this week to increase your level of hope. You may choose to monitor your thoughts and to challenge negative thoughts. For example, the thought "I'll never be able to identify a career goal" can be challenged in these ways: How can I predict the future? I know others who have a career goal; where is the evidence that I cannot achieve this? If I learn the steps necessary to identifying a career goal, it might be possible for me to achieve this goal. When you encounter a negative thought, consider its alternative; for example, by continuing the hard work I am currently engaged in regarding my career planning, I will be able to develop self-clarity and identify possible career goals.

- Commit yourself to taking at least two steps this week to increase your hope. At the end of the week, rate your level of hope once again.

- Continue the process of identifying factors that limit your hope, identifying strategies for addressing these factors and taking at least two steps to increase your level of hope.

My current level of hope is (1 = not hopeful; 5 = extremely hopeful): _____

Factors limiting my hopefulness are:

_____

_____

Two steps I can take to address the limiting factors I identified are:

1. _____

2. _____

One week from now, complete the following:

My current level of hope is (1–5): _____ (complete this one week after taking steps to address your limiting factors)

## Developing Career Flow Competencies

The career flow competencies (Figure 2.2 on p. 14) are essential for you to develop in order to cope effectively with all dimensions of career flow you will experience. They provide the foundation, or the anchor, that grounds your beliefs, goals, and actions.

 Tip    *Use your self-reflection to develop self-clarity.*

## Self-Reflection and Self-Clarity in Educational and Career Planning

### Self-Reflection

Self-reflection involves the capacity to examine your thoughts, beliefs, behaviors, and circumstances; in essence, it involves paying attention to you and your world. It requires the willingness to consider questions such as: What is important to me?

*Self-reflection is the key to self-clarity.*

What do I enjoy? What skills do I enjoy using? What skills would I like to develop? What opportunities are presented to me in my environment? What sort of lifestyle do I hope to have? How effectively am I using the talents I want to use, engaging in activities that I enjoy, and participating in activities that are important to me? Am I living the life I want to live? Do I have a vision for my future? The list goes on. Self-reflection involves taking a "time out" to consider who you are, the life you are living, and the life you hope to live. You should make it a regular practice to engage in this sort of self-reflection. Perhaps you can do this on a weekly basis at first. Writing down your self-reflections will help you to be more systematic and intentional as you consider important questions about yourself and your life.

## Self-Reflections

ACTIVITY 2.3

Spend five minutes on each of the next five days considering any of the questions posed above. Write down your responses to these questions. After the five days, review what you have written.

Consider the following questions:

- What did I learn about myself as a result of this self-reflection activity?

- How does what I wrote about my self-reflections inform me about my future?

As you develop answers to these important questions, you begin the process of developing self-clarity. In this way, self-reflection and self-clarity are linked. Self-reflection involves taking the time to ask the questions. Self-clarity occurs as you do the work to develop answers to the questions about yourself and your circumstances. It is a *process* because the requirement to engage in self-reflection to develop self-clarity is a task that one never completes—it is ongoing and lifelong. Often, you will find it beneficial to engage in self-reflection with a career counselor who can help to structure your self-reflection and provide you with important feedback as you consider essential questions about you and your life.

Tip   *Be intentional about engaging in systematic self-reflection regarding your thoughts, beliefs, actions, and circumstances.*

## Self-Clarity

With effort, self-clarity emerges. In many ways, the process is similar to developing a photograph. That is, self-reflection is like entering the photographer's darkroom to do the work that results in a clear image (self-clarity). Ancient Greek philosopher Aristotle noted the importance of self-clarity when he emphasized the importance of "knowing thyself" to live life effectively. This advice is essential to managing your career effectively. Everything starts from the foundation of self-awareness. If you are clear about who you are, then you can use this important information to move forward systematically and intentionally in identifying and achieving your career goals. If you are not clear about the essential aspects of your personality—your needs, skills, etc.—then it is likely that you will feel somewhat like a boat adrift at sea, subject to the winds and currents that will direct your course. Developing self-clarity will enable you to be the captain of your ship as opportunities and challenges are presented to you.

Unfortunately, many of us prefer to minimize this part of the career development process. Why is that? It seems obvious that it is critical to understand who you are *before* you can decide what career options will fit. So, what might cause us to discount this important step in the process? Perhaps the answer can be found, in part, from the wisdom of Sigmund Freud, who contended that one of the most challenging tasks in life is to learn how to tolerate ambiguity. Humans tend to desire certainty over uncertainty. Many college students constantly switch their academic majors, preferring to claim almost any academic home rather than admitting they are undecided about their choice of major. Denying uncertainty gives many of us a false sense of control over our lives. Unfortunately, this denial often results in just the opposite of control. Denying uncertainty causes us to avoid taking on the challenge of defining who we are and what we want from life. In other words, there is a sort of paradox at work here. Admitting that you are uncertain about your career can often propel you to take the important step of doing the work involved in defining who you are and what you want in life, which is exactly the sort of effort required to take control of your life. Denying uncertainty keeps you stuck in uncertainty, despite any appearance to the contrary.

Trying to make a career decision in the absence of self-clarity is similar to taking off on a vacation with no destination and no clear sense about what you hope to experience on your journey. Most people prefer to identify where they are going and what they hope to experience when they take a vacation. Obviously, making a career decision after having developed self-clarity is akin to taking off on a vacation knowing where you want to go, what you hope to experience on your journey, and what you want to do once you arrive at your destination. In both instances, you are likely to have an adventure. One approach—knowing where you want to go—is much more likely to increase the probability that you will experience joy and satisfaction than the other—not knowing where you want to go and what you hope to experience.

Many of us also diminish the importance of putting in the effort toward developing self-clarity because we may interpret uncertain in a negative way. For example, some people (incorrectly) view being undecided as weak, "wishy-washy," or lazy. Such value judgments ignore the basic fact that everyone (there are no exceptions) has been—at multiple times—undecided about his or her career goals. They also ignore the fact that being undecided is a necessary step for moving from one option to another. No matter the circumstances, moving from situation A to situation B requires asking whether B is better than A. In other words, you must experience indecision before you can be decided—there is no way around it.

Remember: You must do the work to develop self-clarity in order to make wise career decisions. A basic starting point for doing this work is giving yourself permission to remain uncertain while you figure out what you want to experience in your career. Do not interpret the necessary step of being uncertain as not making progress in your career development. Do not be fooled into thinking there is nothing happening while you are uncertain. It may, in fact, be the most important work you do in your career decision making—as long as you use your uncertainty wisely. This means engaging intentionally and systematically in self-reflection to develop self-clarity. To develop self-clarity, it is useful to consider objective and subjective dimensions of your career development.

 Tip *Use both objective and subjective information to inform your career and educational planning.*

## Objective and Subjective Information in Educational and Career Planning

In the area of career development, learning more about oneself often is linked to taking a test. Taking a test can be helpful, and most career centers offer interest inventories, aptitude tests, personality inventories, and so on. Many career assessments focus on helping you identify important self-characteristics—for example, interests and aptitudes—and then comparing your interest and aptitudes to specific occupations. This is an important starting point in gaining self-clarity. It is, however, only a starting point.

The information you acquire from such assessments should propel you to gather more information about occupational options that capture your attention. You can acquire more information through interviewing people who work in occupations that interest you, reading about specific occupations, and/or investing time in exploring occupations through volunteer work, job shadowing, or an internship. Whatever sort of information-gathering steps you take, always process the information you acquire through the lens of the information you have developed about your important self-characteristics; that is, your self-clarity. Ask yourself whether you can see yourself spending substantial amounts of time engaged in the work and work environments related to the occupations you are exploring.

Information from standardized tests typically is reported in percentile ranks and percentage points; for example, you are provided information about your percentile rank for mathematics ability. Although this information is helpful as a starting point for exploring who you are and how it relates to various occupational options, most of us do not think of ourselves in terms of percentile rankings and percentages. More often, we seek a deeper understanding related to the question of who we are.

These deeper meanings relate to the *subjective experience of career development*, which essentially relates to the process by which people make meaning out of their life experience and translate that meaning into career directions. Both objective and subjective dimensions of self-clarity are important.

One strategy for gaining clarity regarding your subjective career experience comes from Mark Savickas, a vocational psychologist. Savickas has popularized the view that early life experiences are essential to constructing career plans. Specifically, his career counseling strategies focus on helping people examine early life experiences, often painful ones, in order to examine how their past connects to their present and informs their future goals. Painful experiences such as the divorce of one's parents are key because they often create a yearning for the opposite (e.g., an intact and secure family). Savickas believes we become preoccupied with these early painful experiences, which cause us to turn these into later life occupations. For example, the child who experiences the loss of a loved one may, as an adult, seek to help others cope with loss in their lives. Coping with loss becomes the person's core life theme in this example. The specific occupational title the person assumes (his or her objective career choice) is less important than whether the profession provides an opportunity to be occupied with chances to express the core theme of his or her life (i.e., the subjective career experience). Helping people understand how they can make meaning out of their life experiences and translate that meaning into a career direction is the goal of activities such as the one that Savickas uses to help others identify career goals.

*Understanding yourself is key to effective career decision-making.*

Shutterstock

## *Preoccupation Exercise*

**ACTIVITY 2.4**    To manage your career flow effectively, you will need to understand what your pre-occupation is and how it may become your occupation. What are you *yearning* to experience in your life? Brainstorm the possibilities by writing them down. If you could experience anything in your life, what would it be? Try to come up with at least three possibilities, describing each in detail. Now, consider how what you have identified may be connected to what you experienced in your childhood. Are there any connections? Perhaps the experiences you identified and the things you yearn to experience reveal an opposite experience in your childhood. Do not be too quick to decide there are no connections. In fact, try to identify at least one possible connection (no matter how silly it might seem initially). Then, over the next few days, reflect on the possibility of this connection.

1. I yearn to experience the following:

   1. _____

   2. _____

   3. _____

2. One possible connection between what I yearn to experience and my childhood experiences is: _____

Understanding how your life experiences can inform your career direction helps you move forward with intention and purpose. In essence, developing this level of understanding provides the answer to what you will need to do in your life to find meaning in your activities. The task then becomes one of identifying which occupations will provide the greatest opportunity to express yourself in these ways.

An aspect of early life experience that can be a powerful influence in your career development relates to the existence of role models you may have had when you were growing up. Early life role models often are individuals—real or fictional—we seek to pattern our lives after. When you admire someone, you often want to be like that person. For example, Theresa identified Wonder Woman as her early life role model. The strength and integrity of Wonder Woman and her courage to confront challenges in life were some of the qualities that captured Theresa's attention. Theresa encountered multiple early life challenges when her father abandoned her at age 5 and her mother died from cancer when Theresa was 7. Theresa tried to approach life using the qualities she admired in Wonder Woman. Later, these qualities served her well in her work as a public defender. Connecting these qualities to a potentially satisfying occupation for Theresa meant finding a job that would allow her to manifest the Wonder Woman qualities she prized. Not surprisingly, she was a passionate attorney who cared deeply about helping her clients confront challenges in their lives.

*Your role models provide examples to follow.*

A woman named Verneda identified her elementary school principal as some-one she admired when she was young. When asked why, Verneda said the principal tried to help others overcome obstacles they encountered in their lives—that was how he approached his job as a school principal. Later in life, Verneda became a counselor (her objective occupational title) to help others overcome obstacles in life (her subjective meaning she expressed in her work). As they were with Theresa and Verneda, early life role models can be important influences even later in life when you are making important decisions about your career direction.

## *Role Model Activity*

ACTIVITY 2.5

Think about your early life experiences, and try to identify two or three people you greatly admired. They may have been role models, heroes, or heroines. Perhaps a parent, teacher, coach, or clergy person comes to mind. Your role model can also be a fictional character.

- Once you identify your role model, try to list ways in which you are alike. What similarities do you share? Write them down.

  My role model was (is):

  _____

  I am like my role model in these ways:

  _____

- Now consider the ways in which you differ from your role model. Write those down.
  I am different from my role model in these ways:

  _____

  _____

The similarities you identified above are important for you to consider in your career decision making. They represent strengths to build on, and they provide an indication of the qualities and competencies you find meaningful and that need to be included in your career activities. They represent core aspects of who you are.

The differences you identified between you and your role model can represent emerging strengths that require further development. They can be labeled as the gap between where you are and where you need to be to grow into your career. You may feel reluctant to engage in these activities because you are not as accomplished in them as you would like to be. However, in many instances, the activities we list when identifying ways in which we differ from our role model can be labeled as developmental skills. These skills, such as public speaking, writing, organizing, and so on are skills that can be developed and strengthened. Unfortunately, many of us incorrectly conclude that these emerging strengths are "fatal flaws" and indications of why particular career aspirations are unattainable. Although certain skill levels may be unattainable, a significant percentage of activities are of the sort that improvement in performance can be achieved with patience, diligence, and practice.

After you have identified (1) your role model(s), (2) the characteristics you find attractive about your role model(s), and (3) the ways in which you are similar and different from your role model(s), it is a good idea to translate your list of similarities and differences into goal statements. For example, you may have noted that one of the things you admire about your role model is her skill as a public speaker, but you may feel you do not possess the same ability. You could translate this gap into a goal statement by identifying becoming an effective public speaker as a goal. Then, you could list 3–5 steps you could take to become a more accomplished public speaker (e.g., taking a speech class, talking to people whom you think are effective public speakers and asking them for tips and advice for improving as a speaker, and taking notes of things accomplished speakers do while they speak). In these ways, you can begin to move more intentionally in a direction that will provide a sense of meaning and purpose in your career activity.

## *Role Model Goal Statement*

ACTIVITY 2.6        Using your similarities and dissimilarities between you and your role model, identify a goal you would like to achieve.

Goal statement: _____

_____

Three steps I can take to achieve this goal are:

1. _____

2. _____

3. _____

Another activity that can help you to learn more about yourself at a deep level is journaling. Keeping a journal provides the opportunity to transfer your reflections, insights, and questions from "head to paper." Not only does this provide you with a document containing important self-information, but it also allows you to create a history of your thoughts. After journaling for some time, you can return to read your journal entries, noting any recurring themes. Recurring themes can represent issues or concerns that remain unresolved for you. Sometimes, it is useful to review these themes with a counselor.

Recurring themes can represent wishes placed on hold for a variety of reasons. When dreams persist over time, their existence reflects our inner wisdom about points for us to head toward. If you think you may have such deferred dreams, you may want to identify one that you could move forward with—even if it is by taking a rather small step. For instance, if you have always wanted to learn how to play the guitar but have never taken even one lesson, you might try doing this and seeing how it goes. The point with an activity such as this is not that the activity necessarily represents your future career direction (although it may). The point is that, in moving forward with a deferred dream, you will learn something about yourself and how you make decisions. You may learn to trust your instincts more than you had before. You may learn the importance of intuition in the decision-making process. You may learn to pay greater attention to intuition in your subsequent decisions. You will also very likely learn something about the activity you pursue and whether it is appropriate for you. You will learn more about yourself.

Life provides countless learning experiences across the lifespan. You will continue to grow and develop. New interests may emerge, untapped interests may be tapped, you may learn new skills, and certain values may become either less or more important as your career unfolds and as you take on new roles in life. When you pay attention to who you are and who you are becoming, you acquire important information that will help you manage your career flow experiences.

## Using Self-Clarity to Envision Future Possibilities

### Visioning

Visioning involves brainstorming future possibilities for your career and identifying your desired future outcomes. Brainstorming focuses on quantity, rather than quality. In this instance, quantity relates to using your self-clarity to develop as many career options as possible. For example, given what you know to be true about yourself and your circumstances, what career options come to mind? Make the list as expansive as possible. Enlist the help of a friend and/or a career counselor as you identify future possibilities. Be creative and have fun!

*Visioning Activity*

ACTIVITY 2.7

• Based on what I know about myself, I can envision the following possibilities:

_____

_____

*(continued)*

ACTIVITY 2.7
(continued)

- Once you have generated a lengthy list of possibilities, identify which ones seem to make the most sense—based on your self-clarity—to learn more about and to consider further.

_____

_____

- From the above list, the following options make the most sense to learn more about:

_____

_____

You may need to acquire additional information through reading, talking with others engaged in occupations of interest, and so on, but once you have gathered additional information, return to what you know about yourself and your circumstances. Always consider possible options in light of your self-clarity. All the information you have acquired will guide you as you engage in *goal setting and planning*, which are discussed in detail in a later chapter.

Once you have identified your goals and developed plans for achieving them, you are ready to implement your plans. Implementing means taking actions that are in line with your plans and goals. For example, if you have engaged in self-reflection to develop self-clarity regarding possible academic majors—and then used your self-clarity to envision possible majors and related occupations, established goals, and identified plans to enroll in a specific major—your next step is to enroll in that major (implementing). As you begin taking courses in that academic major, you will monitor and evaluate whether the major connects as closely to your goals, values, interests, and skills as you hoped it would. If it does, then you simply proceed, pursuing your identified goal. If it does not seem to fit as well as you had hoped, then you will need to adapt your plans (personal flexibility).

Tip     *Develop plans to achieve your goals and revise your plans as necessary.*

Personal flexibility refers to the ability to "change with change and to be able to adapt to it, to be able to take on new roles required, and to relinquish roles that are no longer relevant" (Herr, Cramer, & Niles, 2004, p. 127). The dynamic interaction between you and your environment requires you to be vigilant about maintaining your self-clarity, understanding how your evolving self relates to your career, and responding in an adaptive way to the changes you are experiencing with yourself and your career situation. Acting adaptively in this way requires personal flexibility. In the example above, personal flexibility would entail returning to self-reflection with new information about yourself and your circumstances and then developing self-clarity based on the new information you have acquired.

## Summary

Although there are specific strategies you will need to use to manage different dimensions of your career flow, the model presented in this chapter provides the foundation for addressing all aspects of your career development. Engaging in the activities presented in this chapter will help you develop career flow competencies. As the process becomes more natural, you will be able to incorporate it more readily into your educational and career planning. When you implement career goals guided by self-clarity emerging from systematic and intentional self-reflection, you are able to make career decisions in a positive, confident, and hopeful manner. Such skills will be essential competencies for managing your career flow.

## Questions for Reflection and Discussion

1. Complete the self-assessment activity at the end of this chapter. Score your results, and identify the areas you need to develop. Take at least one step to develop the career flow competencies that need strengthening.

2. What can you learn from Lori Schneider's dream?

3. Apply each step of the model presented in this chapter to Lori's dream.

4. How hopeful are you about your future?

5. What could you do to strengthen your sense of hope for the future?

6. How often do you engage in self-reflection in the ways we discussed in this chapter?

7. Try to set aside specific times this week for engaging in self-reflection about what is important to you, what you enjoy doing, and what you hope for in your future.

## References

Go to Lori Schneider's website to learn more about the importance of hope in goal achievement: www.EmpowermentThroughAdventure.com

Visit this site to learn more about hope and happiness and how important it is in how you live your life: www.authentichappiness.sas.upenn.edu/Default.aspx

Alexander, E. S., & Onwuegbuzie, A. J. (2007). Academic procrastination and the role of hope as a coping strategy. *Personality and Individual Differences, 42,* 1301–1310.

Bandura, A. (2001). Social cognitive theory: An agentic perspective. *Annual Review of Psychology, 52,* 1–26.

Herr, E. L., Cramer, S. H., & Niles, S. G. (2004). *Career guidance and counseling through the lifespan* (6th edition). Boston, MA: Allyn & Bacon.

Savickas, M. L. (2005). The theory and practice of career construction. In S. D. Brown & R. W. Lent (Eds.). *Career Development and Counseling: Putting Theory and Research to Work* (pp. 42–70). Hoboken, NJ: John Wiley & Sons.

Snyder, C. R. (2002). Target article: *Hope theory: Rainbows in the mind. Psychological Inquiry, 13,* 249–275.

# Career Flow Competencies Self-Assessment

Spencer G. Niles & Hyung Joon Yoon

*Directions*

For each item, rate how true the statement is for you using the response scale shown below. For example, if the statement is somewhat true for you, put the number 3 in the blank.

| Definitely False | Somewhat False | Somewhat True | Definitely True |
|:---:|:---:|:---:|:---:|
| 1 | 2 | 3 | 4 |

Please answer each of the following items. It is very important to answer honestly because only sincere responses help you benefit from this assessment.

*Questionnaire*

____ 1. Even when I feel stuck, I believe I can solve the problem.

____ 2. I think about things that make me happy.

____ 3. I know what motivates me in my career.

____ 4. I often imagine possible future events in my life.

____ 5. I have long-term goals for my future.

____ 6. I monitor my plans and actions so my goals will be met.

____ 7. I believe my future is bright.

____ 8. Before making decisions, I reflect on what is most important to me.

____ 9. I know what I enjoy, what I am good at, and what is important to me.

____ 10. I often imagine various opportunities that might be open to me in five years.

____ 11. I have several things I want to accomplish soon to achieve my long-term goals.

____ 12. I evaluate the effectiveness of my plans regularly.

____ 13. I believe I can make a difference.

____ 14. I often think about how my circumstances influence me.

____ 15. I know which life roles are important to me.

____ 16. I have a clear vision for my future.

____ 17. I have specific plans to achieve my goals.

____ 18. I adjust my plans when I need to.

*Scoring Instructions*

1. Transfer your ratings for each item to the scoring table below; be sure to put the correct number of points for each item next to that item's number.

*(continued)*

2. Add the numbers in each column. Your score for each column should not exceed 12.

3. Put your scores in the total sections.

4. Divide each score by 3 and put the outcome in the mean blank.

*Score Sheet*

|  | Hope | Self-Reflection | Self-Clarity | Visioning | Goal Setting & Planning | Implementing & Adapting |
|---|---|---|---|---|---|---|
|  | 1 | 2 | 3 | 4 | 5 | 6 |
|  | 7 | 8 | 9 | 10 | 11 | 12 |
|  | 13 | 14 | 15 | 16 | 17 | 18 |
| Total: |  |  |  |  |  |  |
| Mean | ÷3 | ÷3 | ÷3 | ÷3 | ÷3 | ÷3 |

*Understanding Your Results*

Compare your score with the following ranges and descriptions:

| Each column | What to do next? |
|---|---|
| Above 3.3 | Congratulations! This is a well-developed career flow competency for you. |
| 2.8 – 3.3 | You need to make a conscious effort to develop and practice the corresponding career flow competency. Please refer to the following descriptions. |
| Below 2.8 | Cheer up! Read the following descriptions carefully to find out how you can develop this career flow competency. |

*Directions for Your Improvement*

The following are some ideas to increase your career flow competencies. Practice and/or reflect on these points regularly. Focus on those competencies for which you scored 3.3 or less.

1. Hope
   - Engage daily in positive self-talk (e.g., "I can take control of my life," "My future will be bright," "I deserve to be loved").
   - Identify the positive aspects of your current circumstances in life.
   - Review Lori Schneider's website and reflect on how she managed to stay hopeful, despite the challenges in her life.
   - Identify one famous person whom you admire and then read what you can about him or her on the Internet. What challenges did the person overcome? How was the person able to maintain a sense of hope?

2. Self-Reflection
   - Identify your happiest moments and describe in writing what you were doing in those moments.
   - Reflect on those things in life about which you are passionate.

*(continued)*

- Identify activities and experiences that give you joy.
- Consider your family, friends, coworkers, fellow students, and so on and think about how you tend to interact with them. What do you like about how you interact with them? What would you like to change about your interactions?

3. Self-Clarity
- List three activities you really enjoy participating in.
- List three skills you enjoy using the most.
- List three things that are most important to you.
- Write a sentence, paragraph, or one page describing yourself, integrating important points about your values, skills, interests, life roles, motives, and personality.

4. Visioning
- Consider which life roles are most important to you and what you would like to accomplish in each of those roles within the next five years.
- If you won the lottery tomorrow, what would you want to be doing five years from now?
- If you won the lottery tomorrow, and could do anything *other than what you identified above*, what would you want to be doing five years from now?
- Revisit your desired future scenarios regularly (at least once per week).

5. Goal Setting and Planning
- Set specific and measurable goals for the next several years, according to your important values and vision.
- Brainstorm and make a list of steps you can take to reach your goals.
- Develop weekly plans that reflect your long-term goals.
- Identify one thing you hope to accomplish today and incorporate it into a to-do list for the day.

6. Implementing and Adapting
- Identify one action step you can take to implement your plan to achieve one of your goals.
- Commit yourself promptly to your plans once you think they have been clearly articulated.
- Monitor your progress toward your goals and your plan on a weekly and/or daily basis.
- When necessary, adjust your plans or actions when you encounter substantial barriers or better opportunities.

# Notes

"Success is not the result of spontaneous combustion. You must first set yourself on fire."

—Fred Shero, hockey coach

CHAPTER

# 3

# Pursuing Your Interests (Passions)

## OBJECTIVES

In this chapter, we are starting the process of attaining greater self-clarity. By the end of this chapter, you will be able to:

- Identify your full range of interests—both what you enjoy and what you don't—and analyze the patterns imbedded in these interests

- Use the theory of John Holland to analyze your interests

- Use a career wheel framework for exploring interests in a more holistic manner

## CASE STUDY

Santosh's family moved to America from India about seven years ago. He is the eldest of five children and is part of a large extended family. His father is an engineer, and his mother has training as a librarian but stays at home with the younger children. Santosh has done well in school and seems to be very good with computers. His father has encouraged him to pursue this interest and he is now registered in a computer science program.

Santosh continues to do well in his studies but is not sure that this is the field that he ultimately wants to pursue. While he is competent at handling the technical part of computers, he only really gets excited when he is teaching others. Informally, he works with two of his younger nieces and loves teaching them how to use the computer. His friends also rely on him for computer assistance, and he loves showing them what he has learned.

From a career flow perspective, Santosh is really in the flow when he is teaching others how to use computers. He is patient, thoughtful, and encouraging in dealing with others, and he seems to be able to work with people of all ages.

Zigy Kaluzny/Riser/Getty Images

A major problem, however, is the fact that his father does not want him wasting his time in the educational field as a teacher. His father feels that teaching does not pay well and ultimately many teachers end up being burned out by the end of their career. His mother is more open-minded about career possibilities, but she goes along with her husband's wishes.

Santosh does not want to go against his father's wishes, but he also believes that he should be responsible for his own career choices. He doesn't want to find himself at the end of his career regretting the fact that he never took the opportunity to train others.

Santosh seems aware of his interests and those times when he has career flow. However, he also must deal with pressure from his father. This is a common dilemma for many of us, and it can be worthwhile to think about different ways of handling a situation when differences of opinion exist within families.

*An initial step in pursuing an interest*

istockphoto

## Identifying and Analyzing a Full Range of Interests

This book presents the argument that career flow and the pursuit of one's interests, or passions, is the best option. Dr. Robert Cooper (2001) has reviewed a great deal of the career literature, observing that "research on more than 400,000 Americans over the past 40 years indicates that pursuing your passions—even in small doses, here and there each day—helps you make the most of your current capabilities and encourages you to develop new ones. It can also help keep you feeling younger throughout your life!" (p. 89).

Cooper (2001) goes on to describe a classic research study that focuses on how much money people make when they pursue their passions. In this 1960 study, the researcher interviewed 1,500 business school students and classified them into two groups. One group (1,245) seemed to want a college degree mainly for its potential to earn them more money. The other, smaller group (255) were intent on using their degrees to do something they cared deeply about. The two groups were followed up with twenty years later, and the researcher discovered that 101 of them had attained millionaire status. All but one of the millionaires came from the smaller group of students who were pursuing their education so they could advance their passion.

The career flow discussion is meant to open you up to the idea that discovering your passions is an important element in the career development process. But what if you have more than one passion? How do you identify the full range of passions you can draw from? A starting point is a simple exercise where you take a blank piece of paper and just start writing down all the things you enjoy doing. Don't restrict yourself to work or education—think broadly about your life and what brings you joy. You might like going for walks, or going to the movie theater, or cooking special dinners for friends. Whatever you enjoy, write it down in the space below.

## *Things I Enjoy Doing*

ACTIVITY 3.1    These are the things I enjoy doing during leisure, work, and family time.

- _____
- _____
- _____
- _____
- _____
- _____
- _____
- _____
- _____
- _____
- _____
- _____
- _____
- _____
- _____
- _____
- _____
- _____
- _____
- _____
- _____

*(continued)*

**ACTIVITY 3.1**
(continued)

Now look over your list and add some other things you might enjoy doing but haven't yet had the opportunity to try. Use a different color pen to differentiate these new items from what you have listed on your original list. If you have very few items on the page, think back to what you enjoyed a few years ago. Try to make the list as complete as possible.

Now that you have your interests listed, do an analysis of your top five interests by answering the following questions for all five:

**1.** I enjoyed _____

When was the last time I actually did this activity?

_____

_____

Was the activity something I did alone or with others?

_____

How much planning was necessary to do this activity?

_____

_____

What is it that I get from doing this activity; that is, how does it impact me physically, mentally, emotionally, and spiritually?

_____

_____

What would I need to do to make more room in my life for this activity?

_____

_____

**2.** I enjoyed _____

When was the last time I actually did this activity?

_____

_____

Was the activity something I did alone or with others?

_____

_____

How much planning was necessary to do this activity?

_____

_____

What is it that I get from doing this activity; that is, how does it impact me physically, mentally, emotionally, and spiritually?

_____

_____

What would I need to do to make more room in my life for this activity?

_____

_____

**3.** I enjoyed _____

When was the last time I actually did this activity?

_____

_____

Was the activity something I did alone or with others?

_____

_____

How much planning was necessary to do this activity?

_____

_____

What is it that I get from doing this activity; that is, how does it impact me physically, mentally, emotionally, and spiritually?

_____

_____

What would I need to do to make more room in my life for this activity?

_____

_____

**4.** I enjoyed _____

When was the last time I actually did this activity?

_____

_____

Was the activity something I did alone or with others?

_____

_____

*(continued)*

ACTIVITY 3.1
(continued)

How much planning was necessary to do this activity?

_____

_____

What is it that I get from doing this activity; that is, how does it impact me physically, mentally, emotionally, and spiritually?

_____

_____

What would I need to do to make more room in my life for this activity?

_____

_____

**5.** I enjoyed _____

When was the last time I actually did this activity?

_____

_____

Was the activity something I did alone or with others?

_____

_____

How much planning was necessary to do this activity?

_____

_____

What is it that I get from doing this activity; that is, how does it impact me physically, mentally, emotionally, and spiritually?

_____

_____

What would I need to do to make more room in my life for this activity?

_____

_____

Looking at your top five activities as well as the other activities on your list, what themes can you draw out? For example, you might see that you enjoy situations in which some personal challenge must be overcome. Or, perhaps you need an outlet for getting away from the stresses of everyday life. Whatever the pattern, think broadly about the under-lying dynamics that make the activity satisfying to you. *Note:* It can be very helpful to have input from others in doing this analysis. If you are in a group context, you might want to break into small groups for discussion and analysis.

_____

_____

_____

_____

_____

_____

How will you be able to incorporate some of the patterns you identified with the career/life goals you are pursuing? Are these patterns reflected in the educational and work life choices you are making?

_____

_____

_____

The above exercise focuses on things you enjoy doing, but what happens if you take the opposite approach? In Activity 3.2, you will have the opportunity to explore more fully the things you don't enjoy doing.

## _Things I Don't Enjoy Doing_

ACTIVITY 3.2        These are the things I don't enjoy doing during leisure, work, and family time.

- _____

- _____

- _____

- _____

- _____

_(continued)_

ACTIVITY 3.2
(continued)

- _____
- _____
- _____
- _____
- _____
- _____
- _____
- _____
- _____
- _____
- _____
- _____
- _____
- _____

Take some of these activities and flip them around, looking at the reverse perspective. For example, say you definitely don't enjoy opening packages and putting things together. The frustrating part might be reading the manuals and trying to make everything fit. If you look at this from the flip side, you might say you are more of a "big picture" kind of person and don't really like focusing on the details. Or, maybe you don't like reading the manuals. Perhaps you learn better through experiential learning.

Take five of the activities you listed and determine the flip side. What ideas come to you when you start from this perspective?

**THE FLIP SIDE**

**1.** I don't enjoy

_____

The flip side of this is

_____

_____

_____

**2.** I don't enjoy

_____

The flip side of this is

_____

_____

_____

**3.** I don't enjoy

_____

The flip side of this is

_____

_____

_____

**4.** I don't enjoy

_____

The flip side of this is

_____

_____

_____

**5.** I don't enjoy

_____

The flip side of this is

_____

_____

_____

Looking at these five activities and also other activities on your list, what themes can you draw out? Look at the trends and patterns in your responses. _Note:_ As before, it can be very helpful to have input from others in doing this

_(continued)_

ACTIVITY 3.2
(continued)

analysis. If you are in a group context, you might want to break into small groups for discussion and analysis.

_____

_____

_____

_____

_____

How will you be able to incorporate some of the patterns you identified with the career/life goals you are pursuing? Are these patterns reflected in the educational and work life choices you are making?

_____

_____

_____

Tip    *By examining your interests in a more in-depth manner, you will be able to derive some of the underlying patterns that help to determine your overall satisfaction level. The challenge is to systematically incorporate the patterns into all of your career and life activities.*

## Viewing Interests through the John Holland Lens[1]

Dr. John Holland (1997), a well-known career development specialist, has developed a widely used classification system that can be helpful in analyzing people and work environments. With this approach there is the assumption that there are six different types of interests/personalities that influence career decision making. These six types have been described by Amundson, Harris-Bowlsbey, and Niles (2009) as follows:

1.  Realistic (R)

    People with this type of personality enjoy working with tools, objects, machines, or animals and through this process they acquire manual, mechanical, agricultural, and/or electrical skills. They are practical, hands-on people who focus their energy on making things work. The occupations in this area focus on building things or making repairs.

[1]Amundson, et al., ESSENTIAL ELEMENTS OF CAREER COUNSELING, pp. 12–13, © 2009. Reproduced by permission of Pearson Education, Inc.

2. Investigative (I)

   People with this type of personality enjoy being involved in the biological and physical sciences and developing mathematical and scientific skills. They are curious, studious, and independent. The occupations in this area focus on the scientific and medical fields.

3. Artistic (A)

   People with this type of personality enjoy being involved in creative activities where there is variety and less routine. They develop skills in language, art, music, and drama and tend to be innovative and open minded. The occupations in this area focus on fields where there is some flexibility and the opportunity to apply their creative talents.

4. Social (S)

   People with this type of personality seek activities where they can interact with others through teaching and through offering emotional support and guidance. They are helpful and friendly and develop good communications skills. The occupations in this area focus on fields such as social work, nursing, teaching, and counseling.

5. Enterprising (E)

   People with this type of personality enjoy leading or influencing other people. They have developed good communication skills and can be quite persuasive. They also are ambitious, outgoing, energetic, and self-confident. The occupations in this area involve sales and management, and these individuals also find themselves drawn to self-employment.

6. Conventional (C)

   People with this type of personality are focused on organizing information in a clear and precise manner, and to do this they use their organizational and clerical skills. In carrying out these tasks they are responsible, dependable, and detail-oriented.

*Holland Codes are used to describe occupations.*

Michael Newman/PhotoEdit

## Using the John Holland System

**ACTIVITY 3.3**

As you think about yourself and your interests/personality, which of these types seems the best fit for you? Holland suggests that up to three of these types need to be considered when reviewing occupational options. Rank order your top 3 choices.

1. _____
2. _____
3. _____

As an example, suppose Social was your first choice but you also felt some connection with Enterprising and Artistic; in this case, your Holland code would be SEA. With this profile, you might want to consider working in fields such as social work, counseling, human resource management, special education, being a community organizer, and so on. Once you have your code, you can look for programs of study that match your interests using *The Educational Opportunities Finder* (Rosen, Holmberg, & Holland, 1999). You can also find work possibilities by using resources such as the *Occupations Finder* (Holland, 1994) and the *Dictionary of Holland Occupational Titles* (Gottfredson & Holland, 1996). There is also a wealth of information on the O*Net database (U.S. Department of Labor: www.google.com/search?client=safari&rls=en&q=o'net+online&ie=UTF-8&oe=UTF-8).

List up to five occupations that fit with your Holland code.

1. _____
2. _____
3. _____
4. _____
5. _____

To expand the range of possibilities, you might want to mix the codes a little. Thus, using the example above you might want to consider the following: ESA, SAE, ASE, AES, EAS. By using this broader range, you increase the number of occupational or educational options. For example, by changing the code from SEA to ESA, the focus shifts toward communications. Careers in media studies, telecommunications, film, video, advertising, and public relations become possibilities. As you go through the process of expanding your codes, list at least five additional career options that interest you:

1. _____
2. _____
3. _____
4. _____
5. _____

Tip      *If you see an occupation that looks particularly interesting, take time to explore it further through the Internet or by talking to others who might have additional information about that particular occupation.*

# CASE STUDY CONTINUED

Santosh decides to do some informational interviewing with a family friend (a teacher) and finds that much of what his father told him about being a teacher in the school system is true. He decides that maybe becoming a school teacher isn't the best choice for him, and he takes a position after graduation with a large import/export company where he is working in the computer support division. His job is to make sure the computers are running and stay running.

While it is nice to get a real paycheck for a change, the job itself isn't that interesting. Most of his time is spent in a reactive mode solving various computer problems. He wonders whether maybe he was expecting too much from working life—after all, he has a permanent job, he is getting good money, and he enjoys the people he works with. However, he still clings to some faint hope that there might be some way of finding work that is more in line with his career passion.

Many of us have walked the same road as Santosh. We have found work that might meet one of our interests, but we remain unfilled in the work we are doing. In this book, we suggest that perhaps there is something more (career flow) that we should strive toward. Let's see how Santosh resolves this dilemma.

# CASE STUDY CONCLUDED

After about six months on the job, Santosh is becoming increasingly frustrated. He sees the same mistakes being made over and over again. After a discussion with his supervisor, he decides to offer some preliminary training groups for people in the company. The first group is poorly attended, but the results are good; after a couple of months, the word is spreading that this training is really worthwhile. Santosh thoroughly enjoys the training and soon finds that his job satisfaction has increased immeasurably. He loves teaching and showing people how to get the most out of their computers. Finally, his career passion is starting to align with the work he is doing.

Even though Santosh is working in the computer field, he is now starting to also engage his other interest in teaching, which coincides with career flow. By combining these two interests, he has dramatically improved his chances of being satisfied with his work. While teaching computers in an educational setting was one option, it was not the only way in which these two interests could be combined. It is important to sometimes "think outside the box" when planning a career.

Obviously, when making the leap from interests to options, it is helpful to start by working in career areas where there are good opportunities to use most of your interests. However, the workplace is very diverse, and it is important in this diversity to have a good sense of what interests you would like to apply. Career development is not just about landing in the right field—it is an ongoing process that includes many career decisions throughout life.

## Viewing Interests as Part of a Larger Career Wheel Framework

There is little doubt that interests relate well to career flow and, as such, play an important role in furthering career development. But is there more that needs to be considered? Is it enough to just be interested in pursuing a certain field? A broader framework such as the career wheel needs to be utilized. The career wheel highlights both internal factors (skills, interests, values, personal style) and external factors (significant others, learning experiences, work/life experiences, career opportunities) (Amundson, 1989; Amundson & Poehnell, 2003).

*There's more to career development than just being lucky.*

istockphoto

## Career Wheel

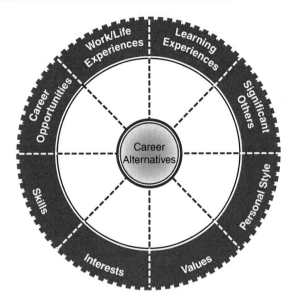

*Source:* Reproduced with permission of Ergon Communications.

Interests represent one piece of the wheel and point toward certain career alternatives, but many other factors need to be taken into account.

The dotted line on the career wheel figure is done purposefully to illustrate that the factors can vary in size and importance. In the case example, for instance, it is clear that while interests were important for Santosh, the opinions of his father (a significant other) were of even greater importance. Thus, for Santosh, the Significant Others part of the wheel might be two or three times larger than any of the other pieces.

The upcoming chapters will reference various segments of the wheel as we broaden the level of inquiry. This is a holistic model in the sense that we only get to the center point by considering all the different factors. In broadening the exploration, there is the opportunity to discover whether a convergence of ideas exists through the various segments.

## Summary

This chapter introduced three different ways of examining interests. As a starting point, the focus was on in-depth exploration of things you enjoy and things you don't enjoy (flipping them around to attain a new perspective). This exploration led to the identification of personal patterns and to the consideration of how these patterns might be applied in other situations. The second level of analysis focused on the more traditional John Holland matching approach where six different perspectives are used to determine career codes, which then could be matched to a Holland code with occupational and educational options. Lastly, the focus shifted to a broader and more holistic model where interests are imbedded in a larger framework where there is the recognition that other personal and environmental factors must also be considered in order to arrive at a more satisfactory conclusion. The following chapters in this section focus on self-clarity issues on the bottom half of the career wheel. These elements include Skills, Personality, and Values.

## Questions for Reflection and Discussion ——————————

1. Can you think of a situation in your own life or in the life of someone you know where following personal interests conflicts with the wishes of others? Describe the situation and discuss some of the strategies for dealing with these kinds of conflicts.

2. When Santosh was resolving his situation, he had to "think outside the box." Have you been in situations where you had to be creative in order to ensure your needs were fulfilled? Describe the situation and discuss some of the dynamics.

3. When you think of Interests as part of the career wheel, how big do you think it is in relation to the other components—the same as the others, larger, or smaller? What accounts for the choice you are making, and how might this impact your future career/life choices?

## References ——————————————————————

Amundson, N. E. (1989). A model of individual career counseling. *Journal of Employment Counseling, 26,* 132–138.

Amundson, N. E. (2003). *Career pathways* (3rd Edition). Richmond, B. C.: Ergon Communications.

Amundson, N. E., Harris-Bowlsbey, J., & Niles, S. G. (2009). *Essential elements of career counseling: Processes and techniques* (2nd ed.). Upper Saddle River, NJ: Pearson.

Amundson, N. E. & Poehnell, G. (2003). *Career Pathways.* Richmond, BC: Ergon Communications.

Cooper, R. K. (2001). *The other 90%: How to unlock your vast untapped potential for leadership and life.* New York: Three Rivers Press.

Gottfredson, L. S. & Holland, J. L. (1996). *The dictionary of Holland occupational codes.* Odessa, FL: Psychological Assessment Resources.

Holland, J. L. (1997). *The occupations finder.* Odessa, FL: Psychological Assessment Resources.

Rosen, D., Holmberg, K., & Holland, J. L. (1999). *The educational opportunities finder.* Odessa, FL: Psychological Assessment Resources.

# Notes

> 66 Nobody can guarantee lifetime employment, but updating skills can guarantee lifetime employability. 99
>
> —*Robert E. Allen,*
> *former Chairman & CEO of AT&T*

# 4

# Mapping Your Skills: Those You Have and Those You Need

## OBJECTIVES

This chapter focuses on the role of skills in career development. After reading this chapter, you will be able to:

- Map your accomplishments and transferable skills
- Benchmark your skills against others who are successful in work that interests you
- Mine your life experience for evidence of transferable skills
- Conduct a gap analysis and implement strategies to develop the skills you need
- Compensate for missing skills by reframing criticisms into compliments

## CASE STUDY

Suki Lo is excited to be graduating next term. Originally from China, Suki has been an international student for six years; she completed high school with exceptional grades and has been an A+ student throughout college. Suki has been an active member of international student associations since she arrived, first in high school and then at college. For the past few years, she has served on the board of the association, originally as event coordinator and this year as president.

Suki stopped by the Career Center on campus to see what jobs were advertised there. Although many of her friends had worked during school breaks, and some even worked part time during the school year, Suki's family supported her financially so that she could focus on getting good grades. Her active involvement in the student associations filled the limited extra time she had.

Suki's goal is to continue to live in the same city after graduation; as she has a work visa, staying in the country is permitted. Her English is fluent, she has made many friends, and, although she enjoyed her visits to China during school vacations, it definitely doesn't feel like home to her anymore. However, she was discouraged to read in the job ads at the Career Center that each of them required work experience. Could it be that all her hard work—her focus on school and her contributions to the international student associations—would not result in a job? How can she explain to her parents that her grades apparently don't matter to local employers? That all employers care about is whether or not she has previous work experience?

Suki's experience is not unlike that of many exceptional students who have focused on achieving success in academics, athletics, or music or committed their time to volunteer activities and as a result have no paid work experience to list on their job applications or resumes. However, lack of paid work experience does not mean lack of relevant experience for a job. The key is to identify measurable accomplishments and transferable skills that will convince potential employers that you have exactly what they are looking for. Achieving greater self-clarity about your skills will, in turn, increase your optimism and hopefulness. Hope is at the center of career flow, and it's important to realize that evidence of skills can be found in school, association leadership, and leisure activities—not just paid work.

In this chapter, step-by-step instructions are provided for mining your rich life experiences, translating those experiences into language employers will recognize, and making a clear and compelling argument that your experiences are equivalent to, or better than, the paid work experience they request. Of course, the information in this chapter is also relevant to those who already have lots of work experience. Throughout our careers, we all need the ability to translate diverse work and life experiences into language that a recruiter, human resource professional, or hiring manager will understand. This chapter will equip you to track relevant accomplishments, recognize and communicate transferable skills, and organize complex information into concrete evidence that proves you have what it takes to successfully transition into work that interests you.

## Mapping Accomplishments and Transferable Skills

An important starting place is to generate a list of accomplishments. This is different from a list of duties, responsibilities, or course requirements. Rather, it documents *outcomes* of your activities, demonstrating your achievements from a variety of life arenas.

Kris Magnusson, a Canadian counselor-educator, developed a framework that may help you begin your accomplishment profiling: the 5 Ps—Pride, Passion, Purpose, Performance, and Poise. In order to achieve career flow, it's essential to recognize your special talents and effectively articulate them to others. Systematically collecting evidence of your skills—for example, in a career portfolio that organizes samples of your accomplishments at school and/or work—is an important ongoing activity. The following exercise will help you get started.

## Accomplishment Profile

**ACTIVITY 4.1**

The following eight steps will help profile your accomplishments. Use the space provided for your reflections.

1. Begin by reflecting on moments in life when you've been particularly proud. *Suki wrote: "It was very exciting to be elected by my peers to be president of the association."*

   _____

   _____

   _____

2. Recognize your contribution to those proud moments. *Suki wrote: "At first I was nervous about letting my name stand for president. However, I spoke to my mentor who helped me see what I could contribute and what I could learn through this. I then formed a small committee to help with my election campaign. I practiced my speeches and even met with a speaking coach twice. I conducted a survey to find out what members identified as their most pressing needs. Then, I developed strategies to address those needs and introduced them in my flyers, in my brochures, and in all of my speeches."*

   _____

   _____

   _____

   _____

   _____

3. Think of your proud moments as stories. For each story, brainstorm a brief title and create a list of your personal contributions, or tasks you completed that resulted in the accomplishment. *Suki called her story "Presidential Election" and*

*(continued)*

ACTIVITY 4.1
(continued)

*listed a few tasks: consulted with mentor, formed committee, surveyed members, made presentations, developed marketing campaign, created brochures.*

_____

_____

_____

_____

_____

4. Summarize a significant accomplishment or outcome for each proud moment. *Suki wrote: "I was elected president of the student association!"*

_____

_____

_____

5. Take a holistic, "big picture" look at your accomplishments. Identify recurring patterns or themes; these likely represent something you are passionate about. *As Suki reflected on her accomplishments, she noticed that she always consulted with others, addressed her skill gaps quickly, and took a creative approach to developing resources.*

_____

_____

_____

_____

6. Reflect on your passions as revealed by your life accomplishments. Identify how best to actualize your passions to help clarify your purpose or career goals. *Suki wrote: "I am passionate about making a significant difference—making the world a better place. I want to work in an organization that is doing something important and meaningful, and I want my role to be clearly connected to making life better for people."*

_____

_____

_____

_____

_____

7. The next step in the 5P model is performance—finding a purposeful outlet for your passions. List places where you used your skills, for example, at a specific job, during a volunteer activity, or in a sport. _Suki listed her association roles._

_____

_____

_____

8. Finally, poise comes from practice. Many of the highlights of your life and career—your accomplishments—likely occurred after you practiced a skill to the point of achieving poise. Record those accomplishments in rich detail to reflect on and to share with others who have the potential to impact your career. _Suki wrote: "I am confident speaking to groups of 4 to 400! I earned 100 percent on three of my recent school presentations, and a local business person who heard me speak at one of our association events invited me to speak at a local Chamber of Commerce luncheon!"_

_____

_____

_____

_____

_____

Tip  _**You may need to use additional pages to list your accomplishments. Consider starting an "Accomplishment Diary," journal, or blog to create an ongoing record.**_

As you share such accomplishments—on your resume, in a cover letter, through a career portfolio, at a networking event, or in a job interview—your enthusiasm and energy (i.e., your passion) and your skills and knowledge (i.e., your performance and poise) will shine through. These naturally exuberant moments of sharing will attract others' attention; you won't need to obnoxiously brag. Rather,

*Celebrate your accomplishments!*

as you were genuinely focused on fulfilling your life's purpose, your accomplishments will speak for themselves. They exemplify flow experiences where your skills and challenges were perfectly matched and resulted in memorable career/life success stories.

You may find it helpful to conceptualize your accomplishments as STAR stories; STAR is a widely used acronym for Situation, Task, Action, and Result. STAR stories will be useful as you work through the entire career flow process, by gaining greater self-clarity, visioning, goal setting/planning, and implementing and adapting your approach. STAR stories may help you connect with your support system, begin to actively network, write your resume and coach your references, generate concrete leads, and respond to questions in job interviews. Therefore, it is well worth some time at this stage to organize your accomplishments in this format.

## STAR Story

ACTIVITY 4.2    Draw from the same stories you used in the 5P exercise. Keep in mind that an effective STAR story does not have to be work related; it doesn't even have to be recent. Rather, the key to a STAR story is that it showcases how your transferable skills contributed to a significant accomplishment. To write a STAR story, follow these five simple steps:

1. Briefly describe the context of your story—the **Situation**. Consider times when you won a trophy or an award. Reflect on thank-you letters, performance reviews, or positive feedback from others. Perhaps there was a time when you made a significant difference by doing something faster, better, or in a new way.

Write down three situations as possibilities for your STAR stories. *Suki wrote: "Coordinating a career fair."*

_____

_____

_____

_____

2. As you reflect on the situations you listed, what was your **Task** at the time? What did you set out to accomplish? *Suki wrote: "Coordinate a career fair for international students, in partnership with the career services office."* For each of the situations listed in the previous section, use this space to briefly identify your goal or purpose.

_____

_____

_____

_____

3. As the focus of a STAR story is your accomplishment, the next step is to identify the specific **Actions** you took in the situations you described and the **Attitudes** you exhibited. Using action verbs, describe what you did and how you did it. *Suki coordinated a career fair by planning an agenda and showing how to set up the space; writing invitations, announcements, and emails; creating posters; and tracking registrations. She was enthusiastic and attentive to details.*

_____

_____

_____

_____

4. The **Result** is the most important part of your STAR story as it represents your accomplishment. Focus on the outcome of your story and, where possible, quantify it. *Suki exceeded the association's attendance target by 20 percent; as a result of the career fair, 30 percent more international students found local job opportunities for just after graduation.* Use this space to record the results of your STAR stories.

_____

_____

*(continued)*

ACTIVITY 4.2
(continued)

_____

_____

5. Some of these action statements may be useful for your resume. To convert a STAR story to a resume bullet, simply combine the specific action you took and the result. *Suki wrote: "Strategically adjusted the agenda and display space for a career fair for international students, increasing attendance by 20 percent from previous year and resulting in 30 percent more international students securing local employment after graduation."* Record these bullets in a master resume—a document where you collect all information that may be helpful for a resume. You will draw relevant information from your master resume when you need to send a resume to a specific employer.

_____

_____

_____

_____

**Tip**     *Use your STAR story resume bullets to get a master resume started; or, if you already have a master resume, add your STAR story bullets to it now.*

Reflecting on the 5 Ps and writing out some of your STAR stories are great ways to identify your accomplishments. Another source of information is interviewing the people who know you best. The advantage of asking others about your accomplishments is that they have a different perspective; that is, they can see you and your accomplishments against a backdrop of others doing similar activities. Many of us underestimate our strengths, believing "If I can do this, anybody could!" We tend to minimize or overlook significant accomplishments. Some people, on the other hand, have an exaggerated sense of their abilities, and are unaware that others have achieved similar or greater results.

Many organizations have introduced a 360° feedback process to help their employees gain a more comprehensive perspective of their performance by soliciting feedback from others—such as supervisors, peers, those writing direct reports, customers—who have observed their work. As you seek information about your own skills and accomplishments, ask people who know you well or who have supervised your work to provide you with specific feedback. Because different skills may be demonstrated in various life roles, solicit feedback from diverse sources such as relatives, family friends, peers, coaches, instructors, mentors, supervisors, and colleagues.

Although you could gather this information through informal conversations, another strategy is to give your sources an opportunity to respond on paper or

*Ask for feedback.*

even anonymously, via an online survey. The questionnaire in the next activity is reproduced with permission from Ergon Communications.

## *Significant Other Questionnaire*

ACTIVITY 4.3

Please complete the following questions. Your opinion is important to help [insert name] _____ make future career plans; therefore, your honesty is greatly appreciated.

1. What would you say this person is good at? What skills has this person demonstrated?

   _____

   _____

   _____

   _____

2. What would you see as this person's major interest areas?

   _____

   _____

*(continued)*

ACTIVITY 4.3
(continued)

_____

_____

3. How would you describe the personal characteristics of this person?

_____

_____

_____

_____

4. What positive changes have you noticed over time in this person, especially in relation to work or looking for work?

_____

_____

_____

_____

5. In what ways could this person continue to improve?

_____

_____

_____

_____

6. What positive skills and attributes have you noticed about this person that might go unrecognized?

_____

_____

_____

_____

7. If you were to suggest the ideal job or career prospect for this person, what would it be?

_____

_____

_____

_____

If you prefer to preserve anonymity or if some of the individuals you would like to survey don't live or work nearby, it is very easy to set up free online surveys using sites such as www.advancedsurvey.com. Send a survey link by email, and use the body of the email to update your contacts about your current status, for example, in school, about to graduate, trying to decide on a major, or looking for part-time work. This type of networking can produce helpful insights and specific job leads. As you introduce your survey, explain its purpose—for example, to help you clarify your career goals—and ask for honest feedback based on the respondents' observations. Your survey questions could ask about respondents' perceptions of your strengths, skills, or challenges as well as their suggestions for possible careers, areas of study, or relevant contacts. Aim to survey 5–10 people to generate enough data for themes to emerge. Request that your survey be completed by a specific date. For short surveys, allowing a few days is ample; leaving the survey open for longer makes it tempting to set the email aside and it may get buried in a long list of "to do" items.

After analyzing your survey results, thank your contacts and inform them about career decisions you have made. This keeps your network actively engaged in supporting your career development. You will likely find the same people helpful in the visioning, goal setting/planning, and implementing and adapting stages of career flow. As an added benefit, their positive feedback and support will likely help to sustain your hope, an essential element at the heart of the career flow model.

Of course, not all of the survey results will be positive; you've asked for honest feedback and question 5 specifically inquires about areas for improvement. Therefore, it's important not to get defensive or take the feedback too personally. Although it can be hard to step back and take an objective look at critical feedback, you will likely find some kernel of truth in it. Learning to accept and value feedback is an important employability skill and will serve you well in future performance reviews.

To supplement the information you've gathered from others about what they see as your skills, review any previous lists of transferable skills that you completed. Quintessential Careers provides a comprehensive list of transferable skills at: www.quintcareers.com/transferable_skills_set.html. O*NET also has a useful list and is directly linked to occupational codes and descriptions; you'll find it at: http://online.onetcenter.org/skills/.

## Skills I Most Want to Use at Work

ACTIVITY 4.4    As you reflect on your skills—using these checklists, your own reflections, your resume, and your 360° survey or Significant Other Questionnaire as prompts—consider which skills you are most motivated to use at work (i.e., which skills are most likely to contribute to your job satisfaction and career success). Use the space below to write down the 10–15 skills you most want to use at work. *Suki learned that she has many skills that will be valuable to future employers. Those skills that she is most motivated to use at work include organizing events or workshops; creating brochures and flyers; presenting seminars; and conducting research through surveys and focus groups.*

_____

_____

_____

_____

_____

_____

_____

_____

_____

_____

_____

_____

# Benchmarking Skills against Others

Once you have identified the transferable skills you would like to incorporate into your career, benchmark those skills. Benchmarking is a method of comparing something to an exemplar or best practice, for example, finding a great example of a specific skill and then comparing your own current level of skill to that benchmark. To begin, select people successful in the field or specific occupation that you hope to build your career within. To identify successful people, consider those you met at career fairs, guest speakers in your courses, instructors, family friends, or people you have seen on TV or read about in magazines. Observe their use of the skills you identified; if possible, set up an informational interview to talk with them about those skills and how they acquired them. For example, like Suki, you may have an identified skill and interest in making presentations. However, as you benchmark that skill, you may notice a considerable difference between an instructor teaching a class at the university, a speaker at an orientation session you attended at school, a presidential lecture, and a motivational speaker at a public event with thousands in the audience. Benchmarking will help you to identify the subtle differences between "making presentations" in each of those roles. How will your existing skills need to be polished or further developed to move you to the next stage in your career?

Some skills are considered foundational or essential. Many governments and employer groups have created lists of such skills and all tend to include basic literacy such as reading, writing, speaking, listening, and numeracy; computer literacy; people skills, including cultural competency; critical thinking skills; and personal qualities such as self-esteem and self-management. As you reflect on your skills, do not overlook the basics. The Skills Framework[1], available on The Partnership for 21st Century Skills website, provides a detailed overview of skills students need today.

## Foundational or Essential Skills

ACTIVITY 4.5

Use the following table to list five skills that will be important no matter what kind of work you may do. Next, identify one strategy for further developing each skill. Use the last column in the table to outline how you can demonstrate each skill to a potential employer. To get you started, an example is provided for Suki.

**SAMPLE: SUKI'S FOUNDATIONAL OR ESSENTIAL SKILLS**

| Important Skills | Strategies for Developing Skills | Ideas for Demonstrating Skills to Potential Employers |
|---|---|---|
| 1. Working with others | Continue to participate in the International Student Association; join an association outside of school | Add a resume bullet to detail an accomplishment from working as a team |

*(Continued)*

[1]/www.21stcenturyskills.org/index.php?option=com_content&task=view&id=254&Itemid=120

ACTIVITY 4.5
(continued)

| | | |
|---|---|---|
| 2. Bilingual | Speak to friends at school and in committees to strengthen English; speak to friends and family in China, on the phone or via Skype, to strengthen Mandarin | Ensure there are no grammatical errors on resume or cover letter; highlight ability to speak two languages on resume; practice responding to potential interview questions |
| 3. Computer use | Take a course to become more familiar with some Microsoft products such as Excel | Add a resume bullet to describe specific computer projects (e.g., tracking career fair registrations on a customized Excel spreadsheet; using MS Word templates to create compelling posters) |
| 4. Critical thinking | Get more involved with problem solving and decision making through the International Student Association | Prepare to discuss specific examples of critical thinking in response to interview questions such as "Tell me about a time when you realized that the traditional way of doing something wasn't going to work" |
| 5. Organizational skills | Create schedules for assignment due dates; use calendar and task reminders in Outlook | Ensure portfolio is neatly organized and resume and cover letter are attractively formatted and effectively organized; be on time for interview |

Now it's your turn; complete the following table.

**YOUR FOUNDATIONAL OR ESSENTIAL SKILLS**

| Important Skills | Strategies for Developing Skills | Ideas for Demonstrating Skills to Potential Employers |
|---|---|---|
| 1. | | |
| 2. | | |
| 3. | | |
| 4. | | |
| 5. | | |

*Use O\*Net to learn more about the specific skills required for work that interests you.*

Courtesy of O Net Resource Center (www.onetcenter.org)

## Data Mining

You've likely already realized that information about your transferable skills will come from many different sources, not just work experience. Similar to other research involving data from diverse sources, it is important to effectively organize, synthesize, and analyze your transferable skills data and then translate them into language useful to a potential employer. Data mining techniques can be helpful at this stage.

## *Transferable Skills*

ACTIVITY 4.6

For this activity, you'll need Internet access to the O\*NET site: http://online.onetcenter.org/. If you don't have Internet access, consider using print resources—such as job descriptions, advertisements, or performance reviews—to find examples of workplace language.

To begin, you'll need an organizational framework. At the simplest level, create a table. In the first column, list the transferable skills you've already identified. In the second column, rename your skills (if required) into language used by employers in your field (to get familiar with this language, read job descriptions that interest you and read occupational descriptions at O\*NET). In the third column, briefly describe evidence of the skill and where you developed or demonstrated it. An example follows for Suki; for this example, we're assuming that Suki is interested in a career in financial management, which her research has indicated is an "in demand" occupation. We have used the O\*NET descriptions for this occupation to translate her skills into relevant workplace language. After her example, use the table to fill in your own skills and evidence.

*(continued)*

ACTIVITY 4.6
(continued)

**SAMPLE: SUKI'S TRANSFERABLE SKILLS**

| Transferable Skill | Workplace Language | Evidence |
| --- | --- | --- |
| Study Skills | Capacity to quickly acquire, understand the implications of, and immediately apply new information | A+ Grades |
| Organization | Time management; project management; setting and monitoring timelines and project progress | Event Coordinator for International Student Association; set up successful career fair; ran a successful campaign to become association president |
| Teamwork | Hire, direct, and motivate project teams; network to develop new business; coordinate others to optimize use of talents | Executive member of several associations; liaised with career services to coordinate most successful career fair in university history; worked with teams to successfully complete projects with 95% average grade on group projects throughout university |
| Leadership | Motivate others; provide direction; evaluate results; coach; supervise | Association board member, including president |
| Languages: English / Mandarin | Capacity to communicate clearly and fluently in both English and Mandarin; exceptional written reports; confident and engaging presentation style | Spoken and written communication; invited speaker for local Chamber of Commerce luncheon; grades from China and the United States |
| Friendly | Customer service; relationship management | Elected by peers to several boards; commended by local employer and invited to present at Chamber luncheon |

Now it's your turn; complete the following table.

**YOUR TRANSFERABLE SKILLS**

| Transferable Skill | Workplace Language | Evidence |
| --- | --- | --- |
|  |  |  |
|  |  |  |
|  |  |  |
|  |  |  |
|  |  |  |

| | | |
|---|---|---|
| | | |
| | | |
| | | |
| | | |
| | | |
| | | |
| | | |

## Conducting a Gap Analysis and Implementing Skill Development Strategies

Through the activities in this chapter, you have likely identified a rich collection of transferable skills that will be relevant to your future employers. However, through benchmarking and reading occupational descriptions in resources such as O*NET, you may also have identified some gaps. Look for opportunities to strategically fill those gaps through school projects, volunteer activities, or paid employment. For example, if you've identified a need to demonstrate leadership skills, just as Suki did, offer to serve on an association board at school or within your community. If your written communication needs practice, offer to contribute to a newsletter and invite critical feedback from peers and reviewers. If you are uncomfortable speaking to groups, offer to take the lead in presenting your next group project or prepare a short presentation for coworkers on a relevant topic.

### *Gap Analysis and Skill Development Strategies*

ACTIVITY 4.7     Use the space below to list five skill gaps you've identified and two or three strategies to build skills in each of those areas.

Tip    *To fill skill gaps, look for opportunities to develop those skills, even though it may seem counterintuitive to volunteer for something you're not yet very good at.*

## Strategies to Compensate for Lack of Specific Skills

Through your surveys, feedback, and benchmarking, you may have received some critical feedback or identified skill deficits or weaknesses that aren't easily or quickly resolved. In preparation for interviews or coaching conversations with supervisors, consider how you might be able to reframe some of those criticisms into compliments. For example, if you are known for doing things at the last minute, you have likely developed strong skills in working under very tight deadlines or working under pressure. If you're shy, you likely work very well with minimal supervision and you're not easily distracted. In the space provided below, list three criticisms and a reasonable reframe for each. In Suki's case, she already knows she will be criticized for her lack of work experience and, realistically, she can't just invent experience for her resume. However, she can come to the interview prepared to provide evidence of the skills she developed through her volunteer experiences.

### *Reframing Criticisms*

ACTIVITY 4.8    Use the space below to list three criticisms that may come up in an interview. For each of those criticisms, write a plausible reframe; that is, turn the criticism into a compliment, or provide compelling evidence of how you can work effectively despite that gap.

_____

_____

_____

_____

_____

_____

## Summary

Suki, the case example in this chapter, is relieved to know she can showcase her rich school and life experiences to illustrate skills that employers are looking for. She has learned to speak about her skills in language that employers use and has organized her resume and career portfolio to ensure that her skills catch employers' attention long before they notice that she doesn't have any paid work experience.

Throughout the activities and reflections in this chapter, you have systematically gathered information about your skills; this is an important step in enhancing your self-clarity. Mapping accomplishments and transferable skills and getting positive feedback from significant others can bolster your belief (your hope) that you'll qualify for the work you apply for. Realistically identifying and addressing skill gaps or deficits at this point in your career planning process provides sufficient time to strategically fill those gaps. This will be much more challenging if you wait until you actively look for work. You can further support your quest for self-clarity by examining your personal style, values, and sources of support.

## Questions for Reflection and Discussion

1. Suki was able to identify several transferable skills despite her lack of formal work experience (see sample in Activity 4.5). In pairs or groups of three, share some of your own nonwork experiences and support each other to identify transferable skills from those experiences.

2. Identify a specific skill you would like to develop. In pairs or groups of three, identify three different ways to develop that skill and the tangible evidence that will confirm you have acquired it.

3. Visit the O*NET website at: http://online.onetcenter.org/find/. Select one job family that interests you and then click on one specific occupation. Read the description. Reflect on your experience so far and on how you could provide evidence of the skills required. In partners or trios, make a case for your qualifications for the job. Provide each other with feedback on what worked well, what gaps you noticed, and how a more convincing argument could be made.

## Additional Resources

Community Employment Services. (n.d.). *Your hidden skills.* Retrieved July 29, 2009, from www.ceswoodstock.org/job_search/resumeskillshidden.shtml. Learn to find your hidden skills by reframing areas for improvement. This resource includes a table with specific examples for what to say to an employer. Too stubborn is reframed as persistent, too extreme as imaginative, and so on.

Macpherson, R. (2004). *How to brag without bragging: The secret to self-promotion.* Retrieved July 29, 2009, from www.yourcareerquest.com/articles/brag.html. This article provides relevant tips, examples, and steps for bragging to enhance opportunities for new jobs, promotions, and raises. Macpherson recognizes that not everyone is comfortable with bragging but says the trick is to think of it instead as taking ownership for your accomplishments.

Palace, B. (1996). *Data mining: What is data mining?* Retrieved July 29, 2009, from www.anderson.ucla.edu/faculty/jason.frand/teacher/technologies/palace/data mining.htm. From defining data mining to a breakdown of the components to an explanation of what data mining can do, this article provides a brief but descriptive examination. This article is a valuable resource for individuals trying to grasp the concept of data mining and how to go about doing it.

## Reference

Magnusson, K. (1997). *Radical change in the world of work: Counsellor's guide.* Edmonton, AB: Alberta Human Resources and Employment.

" We continue to shape our personality all our life. If we knew ourselves perfectly, we should die. "

—Albert Camus

# 5

# Personality Style

## OBJECTIVES

In this chapter, we will focus on personality as an important component of career choice. By the end of this chapter, you will be able to:

- Assess your personal style by combining self-assessment and the perspectives of others

- Understand the strengths and limitations of your personal style

- Understand how each aspect of personal style can be applied effectively, overused, or underused

## CASE STUDY

Melinda and Flo both entered a nursing training program but come from very different backgrounds. Melinda's parents were missionaries, and she has aspirations to become a missionary. By becoming a nurse, she can work in many different countries and contribute to the well-being of different cultural groups. She is a nurturing person and tries to help out wherever she can. Flo was born in Malaysia and has been living in the United States for 15 years. Her father works at a university as an instructor. Her mother died of cancer when she was 12, and Flo has been caring for three younger siblings for a number of years. She is bright and is interested in making a contribution in the medical field.

Melinda and Flo met at orientation and have become friends. Melinda is gregarious and loves meeting new people, particularly those from other cultures. She speaks up in groups and isn't afraid to disagree with classmates or with instructors. Flo, on the other hand, is quieter and more studious. She keeps to herself and is very serious about her studies. She only shares her candid opinions with close friends—like Melinda.

Melinda and Flo are both taking a career planning seminar and looking ahead at future directions.

Career flow is something everyone creates and manages in their lives. At the same time, in order to maintain career flow, it is important for us to know how to adapt to changing situations. This process of management and adaptation is heavily influenced by our personality characteristics. This chapter focuses on personality dimensions and starts with a short assessment process. There are many ways to assess personality, and most of them involve choosing from a list of characteristics and then transforming this information into some form of personality profile. While this can be a useful activity, it focuses only on the way in which you look at yourself. It can be even more helpful to incorporate the opinions of others along with your own self-assessment. With this in mind, go through the five-step assessment process in this chapter. Start by doing a self-assessment, then consult with other people that know you in different settings—in your class, at home, in your leisure time, and so on. Taken together, these ratings will provide some interesting and helpful information.

# Personal Style Assessment

## *Personal Style Assessment*

ACTIVITY 5.1

**Step One: Assessing Yourself.** In this self-assessment, eight personal style adjectives are listed below, along with a brief definition. Take the time to consider both the word and the definition. You will note that all the definitions are written in a positive slant, an indication that each of these personality characteristics can be useful in certain situations. Note which descriptors fit you most of the time. Rank order the terms, starting with the two that are most like you, and continue through in pairs so that you make four rankings. Listed below are the personal descriptors.

**Personal Descriptors**

Spontaneous: I am instinctive and act on my impulses.

Analytical: I am careful, critical, and strive for accuracy.

Outgoing: I am energetic, expressive, and enjoy talking to people.

Reserved: I am sensitive, quiet, and generally keep my thoughts and feelings to myself.

Assertive: I am open and forthright in expressing my ideas and feelings.

Patient: I am tolerant, calm, and willing to let situations run their natural course.

Forceful: I have clear ideas and take action to get things done.

Empathic: I am sympathetic, understanding, and respond easily to the feelings of others.

Here is how Melinda rank ordered these descriptors:

Melinda's top two descriptors were Spontaneous–Outgoing (assigned a score of 4).

She then chose Empathic–Assertive (assigned a score of 3).

Her next two descriptors were Forceful–Analytical (assigned a score of 2).

Melinda's last pair of descriptors were Patient–Reserved (assigned a score of 1).

Now it is your turn to do your own self-assessment:

**From the eight descriptors listed above, write the two that are most like you:**

_____ **(4)** _____

**From the six descriptors left, write the two that are next most like you:**

_____ **(3)** _____

**From the four descriptors left, write the two that are more like you:**

_____ **(2)** _____

**The remaining two descriptors are:**

_____ **(1)** _____

**Step Two: Getting Assessments from Others.** Now that you have completed your self-assessment, it is time to think about who you might ask to provide an assessment

*Ask for input from others.*

*(continued)*

**ACTIVITY 5.1**
(continued)

of your personality. Consider asking family members, friends, classmates, coworkers, employers, teachers, and so on. Try to choose people who know you in different settings. Generally, we recommend giving it to at least three people, but you might want to vary this according to your own situation. Don't show others how you have assessed yourself. What you want to know is how they assess you and how this compares to your own ratings. Make some copies of the form below and give it to the people you have selected.

Tip   *There are many occasions when people will assess you with very limited contact; the job interview is one obvious example. Therefore, it can be helpful to see how you come across to people who are in contact with you for short periods of time.*

## Other Person Appraisal Form

RESUME
ACTIVITY 5.1

The person who has given you this form is doing an individual style survey. When assessing his or her style, it is important to have a number of viewpoints. You have been asked for your input because your views would be helpful. Your cooperation in providing this information is appreciated.

Read carefully the following descriptors and then choose the two most like the person who has given you this form, continuing through the list to the two descriptors least like the person.

### Personal Descriptors

**Spontaneous:** He/she is instinctive and acts on impulses.

**Analytical:** He/she is careful, critical, and strives for accuracy.

**Outgoing:** He/she is energetic, expressive, and enjoys talking to people.

**Reserved:** He/she is sensitive, quiet, and generally keeps thoughts and feelings to himself/herself.

**Assertive:** He/she is open and forthright in expressing ideas and feelings.

**Patient:** He/she is tolerant, calm, and willing to let situations run their natural course.

**Forceful:** He/she has clear ideas and takes action to get things done.

**Empathic:** He/she is sympathetic, understanding, and responds easily to the feelings of others.

**From the eight descriptors, write the two that best describe him/her:**

_____ **(4)** _____

**From the remaining six descriptors, write the two that next describe him/her:**

_____ **(3)** _____

**From the remaining four descriptors, write the two that somewhat describe him/her:**

_____ **(2)** _____

**The remaining two descriptors are:**

_____ **(1)** _____

*Note:* When you have completed this form, please return it to the person who asked you to fill it out.

**Step Three: Scoring.** Listed below is an explanation of how to score the information you collected. There are three calculations that need to be made.

**1.** *First Calculation*—Start by organizing the scores for each descriptor by adding together personal scores and scores from other people. Continuing with Melinda's example, she gave her other person forms to Flo, her father, and to an uncle who was close to her. They ranked her as follows:

*Flo:*

(4) Spontaneous–Outgoing; (3) Assertive–Empathic; (2) Analytical–Patient;

(1) Reserved–Patient

*Father:*

(4) Spontaneous–Analytical; (3) Outgoing–Assertive; (2) Forceful–Empathic;

(1) Reserved–Patient

*Uncle:*

(4) Outgoing–Assertive; (3) Spontaneous–Forceful; (2) Analytical–Empathic;

(1) Reserved–Patient

Spontaneous: Self (4) Others–4, 4, and 3; Total: 15

Analytical: Self (2) Others–2, 4, and 2; Total: 10

Outgoing: Self (4) Others– 4, 3, and 4; Total:15

Reserved: Self (1) Others–1, 1, and 1; Total: 4

Assertive: Self (3) Others– 3, 3, and 4; Total: 13

*(continued)*

**RESUME
ACTIVITY 5.1**
(continued)

Patient: Self (1) Others – 2, 1, and 1; Total: 5

Forceful: Self (2) Others–1, 2 and 3; Total: 8

Empathic: Self (3) Others–3, 2 and 2; Total: 10

Now it is your turn to calculate your scores for each of the descriptors:

Spontaneous:

Analytical:

Outgoing:

Reserved:

Assertive:

Patient:

Forceful:

Empathic:

2. *Second Calculation*—These eight descriptors can be further organized into four major themes using the following formula:

Influencing = Spontaneous + Outgoing

Harmonious = Empathic + Patient

Action-Oriented = Assertive + Forceful

Prudent = Reserved + Analytical

Using this framework for Melinda, she would have the following scores:

Influencing: 15 + 15 = 30

Harmonious: 5 + 10 = 15

Action-Oriented: 13 + 8 = 21

Prudent: 4 + 10 = 14

Now do the calculations for your scores on these four themes:

Influencing:

Harmonious:

Action-Oriented:

Prudent:

3. *Third Calculation*—One final calculation can be done by organizing the scores according to the following formula:

People = Influencing + Harmonious

Task = Prudent + Action-Oriented

Interactive = Influencing + Action-Oriented

Introspective = Harmonious + Prudent

Using Melinda as the example, her scores on these themes would be:

People: 30 + 15 = 45

Task: 14 + 21 = 35

Interactive: 30 + 21 = 51

Introspective: 15 + 14 = 29

Now it is your turn to do this final calculation:

People:

Task:

Interactive:

Introspective:

**Step Four: Analysis.** Now that you have completed the assessment portion, you may wonder what all of this means. As a starting point, it is helpful to look at the individual scores and identify any situation where there is at least a two-point differential. For example, Melinda rated herself as a 2 on Analytical, Flo gave her a 3, her father a 4, and her uncle gave her a rating of 2. It might be interesting for Melinda to discuss with her father why he rated her so high on analytical. It is not a matter of being right or wrong, it is just a different perception, and it is important to understand more fully the rationale for the difference. Because this is a very "rough" instrument, there is little point in dwelling on one-point differences; you really need to have at least a two-point differential to discuss differences in perspective.

*Create opportunities to discuss personality differences.*

Shutterstock

## Strengths and Limitations of Personal Style Profiles

It is important to understand your personal style profile with its overall strengths and limitations. As with most things, it is important to assess strengths and work on areas that are less developed. Think about how these factors apply to your personal life and to your educational and work situations. High scores in a certain area indicate a sense of comfort and ease with a particular range of behavior. Conversely, low scores may indicate a lack of usage of some style areas. If your scores are quite close together, it might mean that you move back and forth between the two personality domains.

### *Strengths and Limitations of Personality Styles*

ACTIVITY 5.2

1. What does it mean to be high in Harmonious, Influencing, Action-Oriented, or Prudent? For this exercise, divide into groups based on your highest scores (make four groups if possible). Consider how your strength in a particular area helps you and how it might hinder you (be a blind spot) in some situations. Also, think of some potentially attractive careers that fit with your theme.

2. Form new groups based on the lowest scores. What insights can be derived by considering this perspective?

It is helpful to consider the relative strengths and weaknesses of the various theme areas. Each style has a certain range (context) in which it is effective as well as some situations in which it is ineffective. Perhaps the metaphor of driving a standard car (with a gear shift) might be helpful in clarifying this process. A driver needs to shift gears in response to different situations—problems occur when we stay in the same gear for too long or when we shift to a gear not appropriate for the situation. Thus, personality is not a fixed entity but something that moves about in relation to different situations. What is important is that we are able to incorporate effective "style shifting." When we are engaged in career flow, we are smoothly and appropriately using the various style domains.

 Tip    *In reviewing your personality profile, focus on how easy it is for you to slip from one style to another depending on the needs of the situation. Effective communication depends on style flexibility.*

By really understanding this information, you will be better able to relate with others. For example, suppose you were in a work situation and wanted to present and get support for a new idea. From your observations and interactions, it might be clear that the manager operates from a strong Prudent style. In presenting your ideas in this scenario, it would be important to outline a detailed and well-organized plan. For a manager with a more Harmonious style, you may need to stress that your idea falls within accepted guidelines and would not be overly disruptive. A manager with a strong Influencing style would be most interested in the overall plan and might be particularly attracted to the marketing possibilities. From an Action-Oriented style perspective, a high value would be placed on the bottom line and measurable benefits.

## Effective Use, Overuse, and Underuse of Personal Style

The last part of this chapter is focused on helping you to better understand how the various styles can be effectively used, overused, and underused. In reviewing this material, think about your profile and focus on your strengths and potential weaknesses.

By identifying areas of strengths and weaknesses, you will be better prepared to set goals for yourself in terms of using your style to maximum advantage. In areas where you have high scores, you will have access to effective use of this style, but may find that you rely too much on it. Thus, in some situations, you will need to change your approach rather than persist when a different style would be more effective. If the style score is low, you have the opposite problem. You may find that you need to embrace this style more than you have been doing in the past. You can access all of the styles; it is just a matter of using the style that fits best for a particular situation.

### Action-Oriented

*Effective Use/Action-Oriented*   When you use your Action-Oriented style appropriately, it can lead to assertive and decisive actions. You are able to speak clearly and take bold steps that require courage and foresight. You have the strength of character to make an unpopular decision and the resolve to carry it through. You rely on your own powers of analysis to sort through the confusion that may surround you. You are a builder and won't quit until the job is completed.

*Overuse/Action-Oriented*   If you are strong in Action-Oriented style, you may tend to use this style in excess and find you are coming on too strong. Rather than a healthy assertiveness, your behavior may take on aggressive tones. You may resort to bullying people when you don't get your way. You may also be stubborn and unreasonably resist any change in your approach. In this mode, you are very susceptible to your power needs and may push ahead with little regard for the feelings of others. You become like a "bulldozer" and, although things are accomplished, you may end up creating more problems for yourself.

*Underuse/Action-Oriented*   In situations where you do not employ an Action-Oriented style when it would be appropriate, you may find yourself unfulfilled, doing the work of others, and unable to follow your own wishes. You may secretly feel resentful, but your good manners prevent you from saying anything. You may also find yourself rationalizing why things are turning out the way they are. Your failure to act leaves you helpless and in the service of others. As a result, you may have difficulty winning respect and be taken for granted.

## Influencing

*Effective Use/Influencing*   When your Influencing style is used appropriately, it can be a powerful means of moving people to action through persuasion rather than coercion. You are energetic and inspiring and confidently express your opinions. You also have a twinkle in your eye and a good sense of humor. This allows you to deal with difficult situations and people with relative ease. You have innovative ideas and can see new ways of solving problems. People are attracted to you, and you have a wide circle of friends.

*Overuse/Influencing*   If you rely too heavily on this style, you may find yourself relying on your verbal skills to get you through any situation. Rather than doing the necessary background preparation, you may push ahead with poorly conceived and disorganized plans. As a result, you leave yourself open to charges of superficiality and inconsistency. When in this mode, you are very susceptible to your attention and recognition needs and may do or say things to keep the spotlight on yourself. As a result, you may overlook the needs of others and create resentments. There is also the temptation to use your persuasive skills to manipulate others. While there may be some short-term gains, the end result is usually negative.

*Underuse/Influencing*   You are unable to express your ideas with clarity and confidence. You feel embarrassed speaking in front of others and are uncomfortable with large groups. You tend to notice the missing details and logical inconsistencies in arguments, but by the time you have carefully formulated your ideas, the discussion may have shifted to another topic. As a result, it is often easier to be silent rather than make a public statement. Even when you do speak your mind, you may find that people don't seem to really appreciate your ideas. You feel frustrated and powerless in social situations.

## Harmonious

*Effective Use/Harmonious*   When you are appropriately using this style, you listen empathically to the concerns of others and deal with problems in a fair and compassionate manner. In your relationships with others, you are positive and encouraging. In stressful situations, you are calm and rational and make decisions in the best interest of everyone concerned. You work to create a harmonious environment, and people can depend on your good will.

*Overuse/Harmonious*   If you are strong in this style, you may be too patient and concerned about the welfare of others. You may have difficulty making "tough" decisions, even if it is for the benefit of the other person. You may also have difficulty being objective and find yourself too lenient with evaluations. You will tend to take the problems of others home with you, and this will be hard on you (resulting in burnout) and your friends and family. In this mode, you are very susceptible to your need to be needed (nurturance). By being too sympathetic and patient, you become ineffective in helping others.

*Underuse/Harmonious*    In situations where you do not use this style when it would be appropriate, you will find yourself impatient and unconcerned about the needs of others. You may be anxious to get moving ahead and do not feel you have the time or interest to be concerned with how others are feeling. You are only concerned with results and can't understand why others don't approach tasks with the same straightforward approach. You are anxious to achieve results and place your emphasis on action rather than exploration and defining the problem. By adopting this approach, you may achieve some quick results but create additional problems for yourself in the process.

## Prudent

*Effective Use/Prudent*    When you appropriately use this mode, you are thoughtful and careful about quality. You are able to take an idea and work out a detailed action plan. You don't get swept away with change for the sake of change. You are disciplined in your approach and stick to methods that have proven effective over time. You let your actions speak for themselves and don't waste your time boasting about your accomplishments.

*Overuse/Prudent*    If you overextend your use of this style, you will find that your focus on details will result in a loss of perspective on the bigger picture. There is a saying that you may "see the trees, but miss the forest." Your need for precision may hamper your ability to act quickly and decisively. Your analysis may take too long, and opportunities will pass you by. In addition to overanalyzing situations, you may be misunderstood because you are too quiet. Your silence may be interpreted as disinterest or a lack of initiative.

*Underuse/Prudent*    In situations where you are not cautious when it would be appropriate, you may find yourself "badly burned." In your hurry to move ahead, you may miss essential details and suffer the consequences later. You may find yourself speaking without sufficient thought and analysis. While everyone likes a quick answer or solution, your "off the cuff" comments may lack consistency and depth. If this persists, your reputation will be tarnished, and you may find yourself without support—even when your ideas are solid.

## People/Task

*Effective Use of People and Task*    The effective use of this style results in a comfortable mix between being on task and being sensitive to personal needs and to the needs of others. You are able to manage your time in such a way that you meet your objectives while still having time and energy for relationships with the people around you. You have a flexible schedule and are able to adjust your time to handle the unexpected. You basically have control over how you are spending your time, and people respect you for not only what you accomplish but also for how you go about doing it.

*Overuse of People/Underuse of Task*    Your enjoyment of relationships may be strained by your inability to meet obligations and goals. You may have difficulties staying on track and find yourself easily distracted by people and new situations. In this mode, you are susceptible to procrastination and insufficient attention to detail. Your focus on people may lead to underachievement, superficiality, and poor quality work. You may find yourself inundated with commitments to others and with insufficient time and energy to meet your own personal goals.

*Underuse People/Overuse Task*     You become so focused on meeting objectives and deadlines that you bypass your working colleagues and other important people in your life. While you may be making some gains in terms of production, you may be taking some losses in terms of personal relationships. People may avoid you because of your inflexibility, bluntness, and/or critical feedback. When people approach you, they may be on their guard and wary of sharing any personal concerns or weaknesses.

## Introspective/Interactive

*Effective Use of Introspective and Interactive*     An effective blend of introspection and interaction allows you to obtain recognition for the quality work you produce. Your talents and personality are visible to all, but this is accomplished within a context of modesty and humility. You openly give and receive praise and are able to benefit from constructive feedback. People appreciate what you have to say because it is clear and thoughtful.

*Overuse Introspective/Underuse Interactive*     Your unwillingness to openly express yourself may influence the perceptions of others. Your shyness and passivity may be interpreted as a lack of vision or ability. You may find yourself taken for granted with few opportunities coming your way. People may take advantage of your generosity and quietness and leave you with much of the work but few of the rewards. You have strong feelings about how you are treated, but it is easier to withdraw than to directly confront the situation.

*Underuse Introspective/Overuse Interactive*     You are very visible in terms of your opinions and actions. Unfortunately, however, you have not always thought through the basis for your arguments and thus can be accused of being superficial and unprepared. You have a tendency to speak too quickly and far too forcefully. People may perceive you as pushy and only interested in being the center of attention. As a result, you may face direct or indirect resistance as you attempt to put your position forward.

---

This chapter is adapted from the *Individual Styles Survey*, by Norman Amundson, Psychometrics Canada Ltd. (1999). Copyright © 1989, 1994, 1999 by Norman Amundson. Copies of the Individual Styles Survey are available from Psychometrics Canada at 1-800-661-5158 or at www.psychometrics.com.

## Summary

In this chapter, we focused on a personality assessment method that incorporates both self-assessment and the perspectives of others. This integrated approach provides an opportunity for discussion of differences between self-perceptions and how we are viewed in different contexts.

All of the personality components are viewed as helpful in some situations and not so helpful in others. Effective communication requires the ability to shift styles, depending on the requirements of the situation. Each style component has an effective use, an overuse, and an underuse. When career flow is operative, a smooth movement between the various personality domains takes place. The image of shifting gears in a car is a good illustration of how personality shifts need to be made in response to the demands of different situations.

## Questions for Reflection and Discussion

1. Even though Melinda and Flo are in the same career field, they have very different personalities. How might these differences influence the career decisions they make?

2. Does a career such as nursing allow people with very different personalities (such as Melinda and Flo) to find satisfaction within the field? If so, how can this be applied to other career options?

3. Suppose two people completed the personality assessment exercise and had identical scores in all areas. Would this necessarily mean they would respond the same in all instances? Apply the concept of style shifting in considering this question.

4. How does the notion of personal style fit with working in a group context? Can you think of situations where your style profile might be an asset and a situation where it might create a problem?

" Your imagination is your preview of life's coming attractions. "

—Albert Einstein

# 6

# Understanding Values through Workplace Attraction

## OBJECTIVES

This chapter focuses on a ten-factor workplace attractor model. By the end of the chapter, you will be able to:

- Understand the factors associated with a workplace attractor model
- Assess the relative importance of various workplace attractors
- Identify how workplace attractors change over time

## CASE STUDY

Jill is about to graduate with a degree in sociology. While she is happy to be graduating, she realizes that her marks are only average and so there is little chance that she can continue her studies in graduate school. She isn't terribly upset by this prospect since it really wasn't something she was passionate about. After graduating high school, she didn't know which major to choose so just followed some friends and fell into sociology.

As she considers her strengths, Jill is pleased that she at least has a degree in something. In looking for work, she is open to just about anything and through some family connections has a couple of opportunities in the pharmaceutical industry.

One of the options is a position in a pharmaceutical company where she would be working with a small team in a sales capacity, traveling to several nearby cities and presenting new products to a list of existing customers. One of the advantages of this position is that she could continue living at home while she gets herself established. She also has a friend that would be starting with her in a similar position.

The other job option is also with a pharmaceutical firm and, though it pays more and has some possibility for advancement, it is not close to home and Jill would need to relocate to a new area. With this position, she would have more responsibility and her own office in a large warehouse. She would be responsible for keeping a record of supplies and ensuring that sufficient product is always on hand for direct sales and for orders coming from sales representatives.

The decision Jill faces is unique to her situation, but there are many occasions when we are faced with similar dilemmas about which pathway to follow. These situations present many complexities, and it is important for us to also think about our values and how these values will be reflected in the decision-making process.

## Factors Associated with a Workplace Attractor Model

One way of considering values in a holistic and comprehensive fashion is to use a workplace attractor model. This approach uses a wide variety of factors (values) and is based on the metaphor of "magnetic attraction" as a reflection of the career choice process. People generally find themselves more attracted to certain career options. There is also attraction from the organization's perspective as the organization is attracted to certain kinds of candidates. In a best-case scenario, mutual attraction would exist between the person and the organization. In this case, there would be many opportunities for career flow.

The starting point for this model is identifying a series of attractors that might work for both individuals and organizations. In considering a number of different models (Herzberg et al., 1959; Holcombe & Ziegert, 2005; Schein, 1992; Plant, 1997; Mitchell et al., 2001; Poehnell & Amundson, 2001), at least 10 different attractors play a major role with respect to workplace attraction (Amundson, 2007, 2009). These attractors are of differing significance for people and can change over time. A brief description of the attractors is listed below:

### Security

Security is a term that includes a broad range of tangible rewards for workplace services. These rewards could include items such as wages, benefits, and travel options. Other forms of security might focus on position security and/or emotional and physical safety.

### Location

This refers to the place where the workplace is situated and to the work environment aesthetics. There may be a convenience issue here as well as a desire to work in interesting and healthy work sites.

## Relationships

This involves the interpersonal connections with coworkers, managers, supervisors, and clients or customers. There is a desire for relationships that are enjoyable, supportive, and fulfilling.

## Recognition

This element refers to the ways in which people receive acknowledgment, status, and praise from others. Some examples of direct recognition include verbal praise, raises, certificates, and other perks. There also are indirect ways of achieving recognition, for example, working in a company with a good reputation.

## Contribution

A sense of contribution comes from work that is meaningful, ethical, and purposeful. There is a desire to be involved in activities that make a difference in society and in the world.

## Work Fit

Work fit focuses on the extent to which work is consistent with a person's existing skill set, interests, personality, and values. A good match between the individual and the workplace usually ensures greater work satisfaction.

## Flexibility

In a flexible workplace, there is the opportunity to accommodate a variety of working arrangements such as working at home and having, flexible schedules, customized benefit packages, vacation time, and leaves of absence. This flexibility often is directed toward greater work/life balance.

## Learning

Learning is associated with involvement in a workplace that is challenging and that encourages lifelong skills development. Workplaces with an ongoing learning agenda support self-development and personal growth.

## Responsibility

With responsibility comes autonomy and authority in handling work tasks. Greater responsibility often is associated with the opportunity to influence others through the application of leadership skills.

## Innovation

Innovation often requires creative problem solving. With innovation comes the chance to have variety, to be original, to employ the pioneering spirit, and to build something new.

# Assessing the Relative Importance of Workplace Attractors

The various attractors reflect an array of positive elements in the workplace. Most of us appreciate having all the attractors in place at our worksite; however, compromises

*Sometimes compromises need to be made.*

must be made in many situations. To assist with this decision-making process, it is helpful to assess the relative importance of the workplace attractors: security, location, relationships, recognition, contribution, work fit, flexibility, learning, responsibility, and innovation.

## *Assessing Importance*

ACTIVITY 6.1

FIGURE 6.1    **Workplace Attractors**

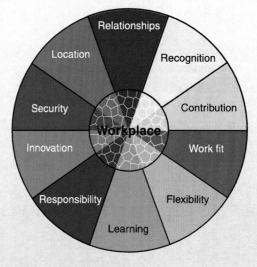

Reproduced with permission from Ergon Communications

How do the workplace attractors presented fit with your feelings about working life and what you consider important? As a starting point, look over each of the attractors and, in the space provided, indicate how you would value each factor as you think about what would be important to you when you start work. For example, security may be important because everyone needs to have some assurance that they can meet their physical needs. At the same time, perhaps you have some family support that might make this less of an issue.

a. Security

_____

_____

_____

_____

b. Location

_____

_____

_____

_____

c. Relationships

_____

_____

_____

_____

d. Recognition

_____

_____

_____

_____

*(continued)*

ACTIVITY 6.1
(continued)

e. Contribution

_____

_____

_____

_____

f. Work Fit

_____

_____

_____

_____

g. Flexibility

_____

_____

_____

_____

h. Learning

_____

_____

_____

_____

i. Responsibility

_____

_____

_____

_____

j.  Innovation

_____

_____

_____

_____

k.  Other (Include any additional points here.)

_____

_____

_____

_____

Tip    *As you consider various work options, you may want to have conversations (informational interviews) with people who are already working in these areas. This is often the only way to acquire a broad base of knowledge about working in a specific field.*

The first step in assessing workplace attractors is to recognize how the various factors are an important part of working life. As mentioned above, however, people often find themselves in situations where they have to set aside some factors in favor of others. This is where rank ordering becomes important, and it is the focus of the next two activities.

## Rank Ordering

ACTIVITY 6.2    What would you be willing to give up if you really had to? Which workplace attractor could you set aside? _____ Once you have dropped one of the attractors, try another one _____, and then a third. _____ What are some of the feelings you experienced when you set certain factors aside?

_____

_____

## *Rank Ordering Using a Pyramid*

ACTIVITY 6.3

Another way of rank ordering attractors is to create a pyramid. On the bottom level, you can place the four attractors that are least important to you. Moving up to the next level, you place three attractors, then the next two, and finally the attractor that is most significant for you. Include your pyramid in the space below:

> In our experience, the attractors that are usually valued highest are relationships and contribution. The attractors that seem most easily given away are security, location, and recognition. In today's economic and social context, many have realized that little work-related security exists. There also is a greater willingness to consider changing locations in order to adjust to new market realities. In an unstable work environment, people know that recognition can be fleeting. The attractors that often assume greatest importance in a climate of instability are those that connect us with others (relationships) and that contribute to a greater sense of personal meaning (contribution). Of course, every person and situation is different. There certainly are no right or wrong answers with regard to the relative importance of workplace attractors.

## The Changing Nature of Workplace Attractors

The workplace attractors you listed help to describe some of the important points you need to consider when making your career choices. At the same time, this constellation of attractors should not be viewed as a static entity. Each person creates his or her own combination of workplace influences at any given time (Izzo & Withers, 2001). This collection of attractors shifts in response to life circumstances and personal development. For example, health issues may play a key role in determining location and what level of security a person is willing to accept. Having children or other caretaking responsibilities might create a greater need for flexibility. Experiences in part- or full-time work can influence how various attractors are valued. Indirect influences can be found through viewing the experiences of others. With the downturn in the economy, those close to you may have experienced stress in their work life. These experiences can play a part in shaping values and the relative importance of various workplace attractors.

*Sometimes a job just doesn't work out.*

## Changing Attractors

ACTIVITY 6.4

List below the ways in which various life experiences have changed the importance of some of the attractors for you. Give at least three examples:

1. _____

_____

2. _____

_____

_____

3. _____

_____

_____

Tip    *As attractors shift, it can be important to communicate these changes to others. Changing jobs is one option, but there may also be other ways of meeting needs through a different work arrangement within the same firm.*

# CASE EXAMPLE CONTINUED

Jill decided to take the pharmaceutical sales position and, at first, was happy with her decision but now is having second thoughts. The friend that started with her decided to get married and soon afterward moved to another city with her husband. Jill also thought that the sales job would mainly focus on existing customers. The reality is that she is expected to do quite a bit of cold calling, and she doesn't enjoy that part of the work. At the orientation, she was with all the sales associates and that was enjoyable. However, now that she is actually doing the job, she is mostly working on her own. This isn't really what she wanted. She is very sure that this is not a good long-term option for her. Staying at home has also presented some challenges. Jill is getting some real pressure from her parents to stay in the current position. Their thinking is that, if she starts hopping from position to position, it will reflect poorly on her reputation as a stable employee. They also have played a key role in creating these opportunities and don't want to create bad relationships with the people connected to the company where she currently works.

The other pharmaceutical position she was considering is still open, and Jill wonders if maybe now is the time to make a change. If she acts quickly, she could give her notice and switch to the new position. She realizes that she needs a change and thinks that it might also be time to get her own place.

As you consider the various factors at play in this case example, it is easy to see that some real differences exist between how Jill's parents view the situation and how Jill views her circumstances. We might also wonder how the employer(s) perceive the situation. What becomes clear is that, in any given scenario, there can be very different perspectives, which can lead to misunderstandings and communication challenges.

## Summary

How can you practically apply these exercises with workplace attractors to your values and to the career choices you will make? Most of the attractors have some appeal, and a key question might be how you will acquire this information prior to making your choices. Usually, the location and security dimensions are easily determined, but it is more difficult to determine the other information. This is where research, informational interviewing, and asking questions in the interview come into play.

The following chapters will describe some strategies for acquiring this additional information. You might also want to reflect on this process with respect to your own career search.

## Questions for Reflection and Discussion

1. Apply the workplace attractor model to the case example. What attractors seem to be highlighted in Jill's situation?

2. What advice would you give Jill as she prepares to move forward?

3. Think about the communication patterns between employers and workers. How might different attractor patterns lead to some miscommunication? Have you ever been in a situation where a different attractor pattern has led to some communication challenges?

## References

Amundson, N. E. (2007). Workplace attractors. *Journal of Employment Counseling, 44,* 154–162.

Amundson, N. E. (2009). *Active engagement: Enhancing the career counselling process,* Third Edition. Richmond, BC: Ergon Communications.

Herzberg, F., Mausner, B., & Snyderman, B .B. (1959). *The motivation to work.* New York: John Wiley.

Holcombe Ehrhart, K., & Ziegert, J. C. (2005). Why are individuals attracted to organizations? *Journal of Management, 31,* 901–919.

Izzo, J. B. & Withers, P. (2001). *Values shift: The new work ethic and what it means for business.* Vancouver, BC: Fairwinds Press.

Mitchell, T. R., Holtom, B. C., Lee, T. W., Sablynski, C. J., & Erez, M. (2001). Why people stay: Using job embeddedness to predict voluntary turnover. *The Academy of Management Journal, 44,* 1102–1122.

Plant, P. (1997). Careerist, wage-earner, or entrepreneur: Work values and counseling. *Journal of Employment Counseling, 34,* 165–170.

Poehnell, G. & Amundson, N. E. (2001). *Career crossroads: A personal career positioning system.* Richmond, BC: Ergon Communications.

Schein, E. H. (1992). Career anchors and job/role planning: The links between career planning and career development. In D. H. Montross & C. J. Shinkman (Eds.), *Career development: Theory and practice.* Springfield, IL: C. C. Thomas.

"If everyone is moving forward together, then success takes care of itself."

—Henry Ford

# Connecting with Others: Social, Emotional, and Financial Support

## OBJECTIVES

This chapter focuses on important sources of support. After reading this chapter, you will be able to:

- Access your allies to support your career–life goals

- Acknowledge the influences of culture, community, attitude, and expectations

- Access mentors, coaches, and guides to help you continue to grow

- Be strategic about your style to manage the impression others form of you

- Recognize the importance of financial management to achieve career–life goals

- Expand and strengthen your network of people and resources, to support your successful transition into the next stage of your career

## CASE STUDY

Pamela Lawson was in the final year of her degree program. Completing her degree had been a long, slow process. Diagnosed with fibromyalgia syndrome in her late teens, Pamela has battled chronic pain, fatigue, and the "brain fog" commonly associated with this disability. However, she has learned to manage her energy and her time and has successfully completed 85 percent of her coursework after 7 years at college. Her marks have been great, but that's largely because she limited the number of courses taken each term and worked closely with supportive faculty, peers, family members, and her medical team. Looking ahead to graduation, Pamela realizes that her success in the workplace will depend on similar supports. Although she has managed her disability sufficiently to complete her degree, Pamela is worried that it might not be as easy to pace herself at work. As she is planning to be married soon after graduation, part-time work may be a good option.

Although individuals with disabilities, like Pamela, face unique career challenges, everybody needs support. Despite the tendency of western cultures to prize independence and autonomy, people have historically thrived in interdependent communities, and many cultures today are grounded in collectivist values. In countless ways, resources and other people will impact your career success and your sense of satisfaction with work and other life roles, that is, your career flow. In this chapter, the focus will be on identifying and accessing practical sources of support that will help you establish and maintain a successful, fulfilling career. Identifying these supports is the final step in the self-clarity stage of career flow. Your supports will also help to bolster your sense of hope as you recognize that you're not alone on your career journey.

## Access Your Allies to Support Your Career–Life Goals

Canadian career development specialists identified five underlying principles that are foundational to many career resources. These principles are generally referred to as the "High Five." They include:

- Know yourself, believe in yourself, and follow your heart
- Change is constant
- Learning is ongoing
- Focus on the journey
- Access your allies

The principle "access your allies" acknowledges that successful people do not get through life alone. Allies are helpful to you at each stage of your career planning and development. They can:

- Share insights about post-secondary institutions, training programs, courses, and even specific professors
- Provide an insider's perspective about careers you are considering (and your "fit")
- Open your eyes to career possibilities that you may not otherwise have considered
- Open doors by introducing you to others in their networks
- Share tips about study skills, professional etiquette, preparing for interviews, and settling into an occupation or specific workplace
- Serve as mentors, sharing insights and tips as your career continues to develop
- Comfort you in times of disappointment
- Celebrate with you in times of great accomplishment

All of your allies are supportive individuals who have your best interests in mind. However, each may know you from different life arenas (e.g., home, community, school, church, sports) and therefore have different perspectives on your strengths and potential barriers. No one will know you as well as you know yourself. Despite this limitation, your allies can help reduce some of your blind spots, emphasize some of your extraordinary talents, and, in some cases, provide clear and gentle feedback about areas you may need to improve or further develop in order to accomplish your goals.

Supportive people in your life are committed to helping you; however, in most cases, they don't know what help you need. As you connect to ask for feedback or guidance, take the opportunity to update them on your career aspirations and progress. This type of networking may even generate job leads!

Tip　*Learn to appropriately weigh advice you receive—and consider the source.*

Not all supportive individuals in your life can or will make equal contributions. For example, a family friend who is the CEO of a company may intimately know industry trends and corporate strategy but have no understanding at all of your talents or personal style and no sense of the realities of entry-level work within the career sector you have chosen. Sports teammates, on the other hand, may know your style well and have a good understanding of how you'd fit within the workplace. They may also be helpful in coaching you about current interview practices. However, they may not have an accurate "big picture" perspective of how the global economy impacts an organization's strategic direction.

## Self-Clarity Themes

ACTIVITY 7.1　Reflect on insights you've gained through "accessing your allies" and from any assessment activities you have completed. Use the space below to note patterns and themes (e.g., did 8 out of 10 people comment on your people skills? your attention to detail? your positive attitude?). For example, Pamela's themes include perseverance and conscientiousness:

| Theme | Sources and Comments |
|---|---|
| Perseverance | Instructor, doctor, and personality assessment |
| Conscientiousness | Volunteer coordinator, group members on school project |
|  |  |
|  |  |
|  |  |
|  |  |

Some of the feedback from others, however, may be a bit confusing. There may be inconsistencies (e.g., one person said you were always positive; two others said that you seemed very serious and "down" most of the time). There may also be a pattern of responses that differs from your own perception of yourself. Reflect on the relationship you have with the people who provided contradictory feedback (e.g., does one know you from school, perhaps from a class you're struggling in, and does the other know you from family events?). The following activity will help you learn from contradictory information.

## Learning from Contradictions

ACTIVITY 7.2

Use the following table to record 3–5 puzzling contradictions from the feedback you've received from others and/or self-assessment activities. Identify the sources of the contradictory feedback and make brief notes to clarify these contradictions. For example, Pamela noticed that classmates tend to see her as outgoing and energetic, but her sister realizes that she tires easily and needs to pace herself:

| Contradictions | Sources and Comments |
|---|---|
| Outgoing and energetic versus Tire easily/need to pace myself | Classmates<br>Sister Amanda—sees me at home after a busy day<br>Notes: When I pace myself and engage in self-care, I have the energy to do a good job at school or work |
| | |
| | |
| | |
| | |
| | |

## Integrating Feedback with the Work That Interests You

ACTIVITY 7.3

To help you clarify your career goals, consider the differences between the feedback you are getting and your understanding of the requirements for work that interests you. Use the spaces provided to reflect on the following questions:

In what types of situations are you most relaxed and comfortable?

_____

_____

_____

What do you struggle with?

_____

_____

_____

What characteristics do people from different parts of your life recognize or comment on? For example, do your classmates see your leadership qualities and your teachers or employer see your attention to detail?

_____

_____

_____

Do you have to make any changes to your career goals to realistically align them with your personal style and strengths?

_____

_____

_____

Hope is at the center of the career flow model. Reflect on Activities 7.1 to 7.3. Describe how self-clarity—having a clearer understanding of who you are and what you have to contribute—enhances your confidence in your career plans and life goals.

_____

_____

_____

# The Influences of Culture, Community, Attitude, and Expectations

Ironically, some of the most supportive people in your life—family members, teachers, coaches, or close friends—may not be supportive in terms of your career planning or development; it's important to cautiously evaluate all the advice you may get. For example, parents may have their own expectations for your career; friends may want to keep you nearby; and coaches may not want to lose a star player.

*Hope is at the center of the career flow model.*

Spouses may have concerns about money, time, or relocation. Although it's important to have significant relationships, they can definitely complicate career decisions.

Some of the influential voices you hear may actually be from the past; you may be carrying messages in your head from previous interactions with important people in your life. Perhaps you promised a dying grandparent that you would go to college to become a lawyer. Or, conversely, perhaps an abusive parent relentlessly told you that you'd never amount to anything. Perhaps a coach, just before retirement, told you that you were the best pitcher he'd ever seen and that you'd be crazy not to continue with a professional career in baseball. Sometimes these voices (even the negative ones) serve as inspiring motivators. However, other times they imprison you. Voices from the past are hard to argue with, even if you now have new information to dispute them. It may be important to access other allies, perhaps even professional counselors, to help you integrate truths from old messages with the reality of who you are today.

## *Voices from the Past*

ACTIVITY 7.4     Use the following table to identify the voices from your past that may be influencing your career planning today (e.g., Pamela's Aunt Tina said Pamela should be a lawyer; if she doesn't apply to law school, Pamela worries she'll be letting her down).

| Who? | Message | Implication |
|---|---|---|
| Aunt Tina | Become a lawyer | Might disappoint her if I don't follow through but don't have the stamina for the long hours required in law school |
|  |  |  |
|  |  |  |
|  |  |  |
|  |  |  |
|  |  |  |
|  |  |  |
|  |  |  |
|  |  |  |
|  |  |  |

The roots of some messages go much deeper than the messenger; everyone is a member of several cultural groups, and members of each of those groups share some common beliefs and expectations. Today's understanding of culture goes far beyond ethnicity (although your ethnic background may well be one of your cultural influences). Also, consider your spiritual beliefs, gender, sexual orientation, age, nationality, socioeconomic status, geographic location—really, any contextual factors that may have shaped your beliefs and expectations. As you complete the following activity, reflect on cultural traditions that have influenced you (e.g., are important decisions made independently, discussed with the family, or made only after consultation with elders or spiritual advisors?). Who will you involve in your career decision?

## *The Impact of Culture*

ACTIVITY 7.5    Use the table provided on page 104 to identify some of the cultural groups you identify with and the messages about career that those cultural affiliations have influenced (e.g., Pamela's spiritual beliefs motivate her to provide community service; for others, cultural influences could include an immigrant family's belief that education is the key to success or the perception of limited job opportunities in a rural community).

*(continued)*

ACTIVITY 7.5
(continued)

| Cultural Group | Message | Implication |
|---|---|---|
| Church | Community service | Perhaps work in a social services setting |
| | | |
| | | |
| | | |
| | | |
| | | |
| | | |
| | | |
| | | |
| | | |

A specific subculture is your immediate family. If you are in a committed relationship, it can be complicated to juggle two careers concurrently. Dual career couples often find it challenging to decide whose career will come first at career crossroads. For example, if one gets an amazing job offer that requires relocation, is the other prepared to give up his/her job? If one has to work overtime to meet a deadline, will the other be able to arrange to pick children up from daycare?

istockphoto

*At career crossroads, dual career couples often find it challenging to decide whose career will come first.*

## *The Impact of Relationships on Careers*

**ACTIVITY 7.6**    If you are in a committed relationship, or expect to be in one as your career develops, use the space below to consider how this may impact the career you are considering and, in turn, how that type of career may impact your relationship. For example, Pamela is looking forward to a long-awaited marriage soon after graduation. Financially, this will likely mean that part-time work will meet their financial needs.

_____

_____

_____

_____

_____

As we've discussed throughout this book, hope is at the center of the career flow model. In previous research, optimism was discovered to be the single best predictor of both career success and job satisfaction (Neault, 2002). Optimistic people are resilient. One dictionary definition of resilience is "cheerful buoyancy"—what a great fit for career flow! Optimistic people tend to have faith in the future, a sense that things will work out. They tend to believe in their industry and organization; they also believe in themselves.

**Tip**    *Optimism is linked to career success and job satisfaction. A positive attitude and a spirit of hopefulness can significantly impact your career flow.*

## *Hope for the Future*

**ACTIVITY 7.7**    A positive attitude makes a very important contribution to personal development. Lack of hope, on the other hand, can unnecessarily restrict career opportunities. Without hope, you may not strive for advanced education or a more challenging job. Use the space provided to reflect on what you hope for in the next stages of your

*(continued)*

ACTIVITY 7.7
(continued)

career–life journey. For example, Pamela hopes to find work that makes a significant difference to her community—work that is manageable with her disability.

_____

_____

_____

_____

_____

Employers also value a positive attitude. In countless surveys, employers emphasize "soft skills" as essential to career success. Such attributes include interpersonal skills (getting along with people), initiative (being proactive), adaptability (changing direction or making adjustments when necessary), diligence (getting the job done), creativity (thinking of new approaches or solutions), and honesty. However, near the top of most employer survey results is an enthusiastic, positive attitude. Employers want staff and managers who bring positive energy to the workplace—people who are engaging and inspiring.

## Staying Positive at Work

ACTIVITY 7.8

Use the space provided in the table below to identify ten ways to keep your attitude positive. For each, identify a tangible way to demonstrate your positive attitude at work. For example, Pamela realizes that getting enough rest is essential for her to stay positive during the day.

|    | Strategies for Staying Positive | Evidence in the Workplace |
|----|----------------------------------|----------------------------|
|    | Getting enough rest | Energetic contributions, enthusiasm |
| 1  |  |  |
| 2  |  |  |
| 3  |  |  |
| 4  |  |  |
| 5  |  |  |
| 6  |  |  |
| 7  |  |  |
| 8  |  |  |
| 9  |  |  |
| 10 |  |  |

Despite your best intentions, it can be hard to stay positive when your expectations collide with the workplace reality. It's frustrating to be hired for your education and experience but then expected to do mundane tasks at work. It's disappointing to be promised a promotion but have it put on hold due to changes in the economy, or because the person you were to replace decided not to retire when expected. It's discouraging, especially when you always got great marks at school, to try your very best at work but constantly get feedback that your best simply isn't good enough.

Achieving and sustaining career flow requires managing your attitude and expectations. Keep your destination in mind and make the small daily adjustments necessary to keep your attitude upbeat and your expectations aligned with the realities of the workplace and the local and global economies. Victor Frankl, under the toughest of circumstances while he was in a Nazi prison in World War II, reflected on "the last of the human freedoms—to choose one's attitude in any given set of circumstances, to choose one's own way." You, too, can choose your attitude as you continue on your career journey. Sometimes, you'll need support from mentors, coaches, or guides to keep your attitude positive and your journey on track. The next section discusses the supports that people like these can offer.

## Access Mentors, Coaches, and Guides to Help You Continue to Grow

The terms *mentors, coaches*, and *guides* are sometimes used interchangeably. Here, however, *mentors* are generally helpful to your career development but aren't positioned to provide specific coaching or skill development. You may have formal or informal relationships with your mentors (e.g., you may be formally assigned a mentor through a program at school or through a professional association, or you may informally ask an acquaintance to be your mentor). In some cases, the relationship may be so informal that the mentor doesn't even know he or she is serving that role; an example would be a leader in the field you are watching from afar. You can learn a lot from a mentor through observation, research (finding his or her resume or bio online), and benchmarking (comparing your current level of skills and experience to the level the mentor has achieved to be successful).

## *Identify Potential Mentors*

ACTIVITY 7.9

The next three steps will help you identify individuals who would be suitable candidates for the role of mentor and who could contribute to your career success.

1. Take a moment to identify the characteristics you would like in a mentor, such as a good listener, an expert at _____, connected to _____ industry, and so on.
2. Next, identify sources for potential mentors such as college mentorship programs, professional associations, and so on.
3. Finally, if you already have a mentor in mind, name him or her and set some specific goals to work on with your mentor's support.

*(continued)*

ACTIVITY 7.9
(continued)

1. Mentor Characteristics

_____

_____

_____

_____

_____

2. Potential Sources of Mentors

_____

_____

_____

_____

3. Specific Possibilities and Goals to Work on Together

_____

_____

_____

_____

_____

## *Identify Potential Coaches*

ACTIVITY 7.10    The term *coach* is used here to describe a slightly different role than a mentor. Generally, coaches have the opportunity to observe you in action and provide specific feedback that will help you develop work-related skills and attitudes. Use the space in the table provided to identify three specific skills that a coach might be able to help you with. Beside each, identify who might be able to coach you (consider friends, colleagues, instructors, supervisors, or other trusted allies). To get you started, an example is completed for Pamela.

| Skill or Attitude | Potential Coach |
|---|---|
| Time management skills, meeting deadlines | Dr. Lee Harmond (English 1104 professor) |
| | |
| | |

*Coaches help you develop work-related skills and attitudes.*

## *Accessing Guidance*

ACTIVITY 7.11

*Guides*, on the other hand, may include anyone who provides you with wisdom and sound advice. Members of some cultural communities consult elders before making big decisions; members of other communities consult spiritual advisors. Parents and older siblings guide many career decisions. Within the workplace, leaders of professional associations, speakers, instructors and professors, labor market analysts, economists, authors, and journalists all provide career-related guidance. Within the community service and educational systems, career counselors and academic advisors may serve as guides. Use the table below to list specific questions you have at this stage of your career journey. Identify two or three potential guides (or sources of guidance) for each of your questions. The example provided relates to Pamela's concerns about managing to cope with her disability after she graduates and enters the workforce.

| Question | Potential Guides/Sources of Guidance |
| --- | --- |
| Is it possible to find work that is flexible enough to accommodate my illness? | Check with the Fibromyalgia Association to see if there's someone I can speak to; contact HR in two large organizations to see if they have any success stories |
|  |  |
|  |  |
|  |  |
|  |  |

## Strategic Impression Management

Mentors, coaches, and guides may all be useful sources of support as you prepare to create a positive first impression with those who will impact your career progress. Every industry, region, and organization has unwritten rules about "the way things are done around here." Similar to having an instructor or guide advise you about the right equipment for whitewater rafting, it's important to know how to network effectively, dress appropriately, and speak and write in a way that fits your audience. There isn't a "one size fits all" approach to this, despite the proliferation of articles and self-help books on the topic. As you transition from school to work, between careers, or into increasing responsibilities within your current organization, consider everything that contributes to the first impression others form about you.

# Impression Management

**ACTIVITY 7.12**

Use the following table as you consider changes you may need to make as you prepare for the next stage in your career (e.g., shifting from full-time student status to applying for full-time work post-graduation). If the item is contributing to a positive impression, put a checkmark in the "recommended change column." If it has the potential to create a negative impression, list a recommended change in the space provided.

| Item | Recommended Change |
| --- | --- |
| Email address | |
| Voicemail message (landline) | |
| Voicemail message (mobile) | |
| Online presence (Facebook) | |
| Online presence (personal webpage) | |
| Online presence (other) | |
| Accessories (jewelery/watch) | |
| Accessories (bag/briefcase) | |
| Hair (cut, color) | |
| Fingernails (and toenails if wearing open-toed shoes) | |
| Clothing (Tip: Aim to dress for the position one level above the one you are applying for) | |
| Shoes | |
| Outerwear | |
| Level of language | |
| Spelling/grammar | |
| Email abbreviations (Tip: Reserve casual abbreviations such as TTFN, LOL, or ROFL for family and friends) | |
| Etiquette (formality, manners, appropriate follow-up) | |

Keep in mind that "impression management" is not about creating a fake persona. We all have different types of clothes in our closet that we wear for specific purposes. Impression management is simply about being intentional—choosing when and for which purpose to share different aspects of who we are.

In the case of disability, such as Pamela in our example, it will be important to decide if, when, or how to disclose. Strategic disclosure—giving adequate information to the people who need it—is important; mentors, coaches, or guides may be helpful in developing a disclosure strategy. Culture audits, which involve observing potential organizations in person or online to detect their diversity, may be useful in determining how to approach disclosure. In some cases, letting a potential or new employer know about a disability is required in order to arrange accommodations. For example, Pamela may need a shorter work week or the opportunity to take longer rest breaks during the day. In other cases, early disclosure may lead to real or perceived discrimination: If Pamela disclosed her disability during an interview and then didn't get the job simply because she wasn't the most qualified candidate, it might seem that she wasn't hired because of her disability. However, choosing not to disclose could result in misunderstandings after she's hired if it becomes apparent that she can't manage the everyday demands of the job to the same extent as other employees.

## The Influence of Financial Management on Achieving Career–Life Goals

Career transitions may require extra financial support upfront and, especially in the case of post-graduation careers or promotions, may bring with them a significant increase in financial resources. If you acquired student loans while preparing for your career, be sure you are completely familiar with repayment requirements and options. If you have debt from multiple sources, such as credit cards or car loans, consider speaking with your banker about a consolidation loan to organize your finances more efficiently and, in some cases, reduce your interest payments.

As you prepare for your post-college job search, carefully distinguish between wants and needs. For example, you may *need* an outfit for interviews and networking events; you may *want* something new with a designer label and may *not want* to wear the same outfit to several different events. Chances are, your contacts will not notice that you've worn the same basic outfit more than once as long as it's appropriate and it looks neat and clean.

Job searching may require some investment in travel as well, whether local (resulting in increased fuel or transit costs) or further afield (requiring flights and accommodation). Look ahead and begin to save, or find a viable source of support, for such expenses.

## *Job Search/Post-Graduation Expenses*

ACTIVITY 7.13    Use the space provided in the table to jot down your anticipated job search and post-graduation-related expenses. Consider where money will come from to cover those costs. For example, Pamela realizes she doesn't have any clothes suitable for a job interview.

| Item | Cost | Source of $ |
|---|---|---|
| Interview outfit (jacket, pants, shoes, bag) | $150 | Birthday gift from parents |
|  |  |  |
|  |  |  |
|  |  |  |
|  |  |  |
|  |  |  |
|  |  |  |

Once you've secured the position of your dreams, be strategic about allocating salary increases; if you have become used to living on less, a new job or promotion can offer a great opportunity to pay down debts or add to savings.

## Strengthening Your Supports

Whether for social, emotional, or financial support, most people rely on others. As previously discussed, strategic networking can help to build and sustain the supports you'll need. Sometimes, however, you'll need supports beyond what your networks can offer. Don't overlook the myriad of community agencies and organizations that can offer practical support when you need it; for example, www.iSafetyNet.org serves as a national clearinghouse for community resources across the United States.

Depending on your need for support, consider joining associations (community-based or professional) or support groups. There's often a synergy in groups that causes the whole to become significantly stronger than the sum of its individual parts.

It's important to acknowledge that your need for learning will be lifelong; that is, your education won't be done just because you graduate. Therefore, as you expand your sources of support, consider what future education or training you might need to sustain your career success.

## Summary

In the opening case study and through many of the activities, we shared Pamela Lawson's story. Pamela is close to successfully completing school, but it has taken her considerably longer than most and she has been successful largely because of supportive family and friends and accommodating instructors and college administrators. In order to experience similar success within the workplace, Pamela will need to ensure that she continues to have supports in place. You, too, will need supports—we all do!

This chapter has provided information about accessing your allies and soliciting feedback from those who know you well. You have considered the impact of culture, community, attitude, and expectations. You were encouraged to consider who might serve as mentors, coaches, and guides as you continue your career journey and to reflect on the importance of impression management and financial management.

Toward the end of this chapter, the emphasis was on expanding your supports and committing to lifelong learning. Use the questions below to reflect on your learning from this chapter and take it to a deeper level through discussion. Within the career flow model, after you get clear about who you are and what you'll need to succeed, the next stages include visioning and goal setting. With self-clarity and supports in place, you are ready to move on to envisioning a career path that fits you.

## Questions for Reflection and Discussion

1. Reflect on Pamela Lawson's story, shared in the opening case study. In groups of three, discuss the kinds of supports she may need to make a successful school-to-work transition and how to put such supports in place.

2. Write down a specific question you have about transitioning from school to work. Some examples include: What do I wear to a Chamber of Commerce networking event? When do I have to start paying back student loans? What professional associations should I join as a [name the occupation]? What is a good local source of high-quality, inexpensive, business casual clothes?
   a. Form pairs and try to answer each other's questions.
   b. After two minutes, form new pairs and repeat the process.
   c. Do this five times, then report back to the larger group about what sources of support you identified within the room.
   Discuss how a similar approach—such as asking specific questions and asking people in your existing network to respond—might help as you prepare for the next stage on your career journey.

3. Impression management can be a touchy, and potentially offensive, topic. Consider some of your personal reactions as you contemplated changing aspects of yourself in order to assist others to create a positive first impression of you. In small groups, share those reactions and offer different perspectives as you support each other to consider this challenging subject.

## Additional Resources

The Portsmouth Group, Inc. (2009). *iSafetyNet Community, Health, Social & Spiritual Resources.* Retrieved July 29, 2009, from www.isafetynet.org/default.asp. This website lists various community resources (both public and private). There are several links for visitors to navigate to the appropriate organization.

Rich, P. (1999). *Giving and receiving feedback.* Retrieved July 30, 2009, from www.selfhelpmagazine.com/articles/growth/feedback.html. This website provides tips for effective feedback.

Rosenberg McKay, D. (n.d.). *Why you should have a mentor.* Retrieved July 30, 2009, from http://careerplanning.about.com/od/workplacesurvival/a/mentor.htm. This website elaborates on the significant impact a mentor could have on your career success.

## Reference

Neault, R. (2002). Thriving in the new millennium: Career management in the changing world of work. *Canadian Journal of Career Development, 1(1), 11–21.*

" Your goals are the road maps that guide you and show you what is possible for your life. "

—Les Brown

# 8

# Optimal Career Flow and Setting Goals

## OBJECTIVES

This chapter introduces you to the importance of optimal career flow experiences and goal setting. After reading this chapter, you will be able to:

- Describe the concept of optimal career flow
- Increase the probability of optimal career flow occurring in your life
- Understand the importance of a vision statement
- Engage in brainstorming to create a vision of future career possibilities
- Create a personal vision statement
- Use a SMART goal-setting strategy
- Understand the importance of planning, implementing, and adapting

## CASE STUDY

Daryll is a senior majoring in elementary education. Currently, he is doing his student teaching in an urban school located in an economically challenged part of a city in the northeastern United States. He is teaching fourth grade students. The student body is comprised largely of African American students. Many of the students come from single-parent families. Daryll loves the work he is doing. Although it is often challenging, he has a strong sense of commitment to his students. He often notices how the students' circumstances remind him of his own when he was their age.

Daryll's parents were divorced and his mother worked two jobs to provide for Daryll and his younger brother. Although his circumstances were challenging, Daryll had support from his mother and his grandmother (who also lived with his family). He believes that it was the support they gave him that helped him make good decisions about his friends and his activities. Daryll was also exposed to caring teachers during his elementary school years. His teachers helped him to believe in himself and taught him the value of hard work. They exposed him to a variety of activities that helped him develop his interests. They also provided him with the opportunity to serve as a mentor to younger students, which was something he began as a fifth grader and continued until he graduated from high school. His teachers often remarked that Daryll was a "natural teacher."

Daryll enjoys many things about his student teaching experience. He loves preparing lessons that he hopes will motivate and inspire his students. In the evening, his roommates often notice how much time Daryll spends preparing his lesson plans. Daryll is typically surprised when they comment about this because, to him, it seems like the time has flown by very quickly. Daryll also enjoys working with students one-on-one. He enjoys helping individual students who are struggling with a homework assignment. He often finds creative ways to help them overcome learning challenges. In talking with his supervising teacher, Daryll mentioned how lucky he feels that he is able to make a difference in the lives of his students. At times, he is amazed that he will soon be paid for doing something he loves so much.

The term *flow* comes from the work of leading psychologist Mihaly Csikszentmihalyi, who coined the term after interviewing a large number of people to try to understand their experience of being totally immersed in an activity—"in the zone," as they say. He found clear patterns among people who experience being in the flow. Learning about these patterns can help people focus their activities in ways that can increase the probability of having a flow experience, something most people describe as highly desirable.

## Defining Optimal Career Flow

Because we focus on career planning in this book, we use the term *optimal career flow* to describe the experience of being totally immersed in a work-related activity. By focusing on optimal career flow in your life, you can identify the work activities you are most likely to find highly satisfying. Although no job is highly satisfying 100 percent of the time, it makes sense to make educational and career plans that direct you toward an occupation that will be very enjoyable most of the time—one that will provide the greatest possibilities for experiencing optimal career flow.

Drawing on the work of Csikszentmihalyi, you increase the likelihood of experiencing optimal career flow by participating in work tasks you find meaningful and appropriately challenging. Additionally, there must be clear goals for the task, and you must receive accurate feedback regarding your task performance. It is important to note that optimal career flow is task-specific. Each occupation requires a person to perform a wide variety of tasks. Some tasks will be more desirable than others. In our jobs as university professors, for example, we may feel optimal career flow as we write the chapters of this book but not when we meet with a committee on which we reluctantly agreed to serve. Both tasks, however, are part of our jobs as university professors. It is the task we are engaged in that makes the difference relative to our opportunities to experience optimal career flow.

An important aspect of optimal career flow relates to the challenge level of a task. If the challenge of the task is too great for your skill level, you will feel overwhelmed. If you find that the challenges involved in completing the task are below your skill level, you will become bored with the task. Thus, the challenge of the task must be significant but not beyond your capacity to complete successfully.

When asked to describe how they felt when they experienced optimal career flow, interviewees responded with the following comments:

I had lots of energy!

I was in tune with what I was doing.

Time flew!

I had a sense of belonging.

I had a sense of connectedness.

I experienced a sense of intimacy with the activity.

I felt invigorated.

I felt as though I wanted to share with others.

I felt a sense of passion.

I had a feeling of being in alignment.

I had the sense that this is what life should be about.

I felt connected to something bigger.

I felt that I was bringing myself into my work.

I wasn't thinking, I was just doing or being.

Clearly, people describe very powerful and desirable emotions when they focus on optimal career flow experiences. Interestingly, the descriptions above relate to what Csikszentmihalyi found in his research. Specifically, he noted that when experiencing flow, people often state that they feel a sense of purpose and passion in their activities. They have a real sense of joy. There often is the feeling that "time flew by" while they were engaged in a specific task. When people experience flow, they have a personal investment in what they are doing and experience a connection with the tasks in which they are engaged.

*Do what you love and love what you do.*

## Optimal Career Flow Assessment

ACTIVITY 8.1

To learn more about optimal career flow in your life, it will help to pay attention to the emotional experiences you have when you engage in a variety of tasks. By focusing your attention in this way, you can begin to increase your awareness of the types of tasks that tend to be associated with experiencing optimal career flow for you. You can begin this process by considering the following questions.

- Which activities would you choose to engage in if you could engage in any activities you wanted to? Why?

  _____

- If you woke up tomorrow and could be doing whatever you wanted to do, what would you be doing?

  _____

- How would you spend your time?

  _____

- What do you enjoy about these activities?

  _____

## Increasing the Probability of Optimal Career Flow

Csikszentmihalyi (1988) found that optimal flow experiences tend to occur more at work than in leisure activities. Csikszentmihalyi stated that this finding is not surprising because work life tends to be more structured than leisurely. Specifically, in work, there are typically performance goals, performance expectations, and feedback. It is also true that work tends to require concentration and engages a person's skills in task behavior. These are all keys for having optimal career flow experiences.

You might wonder about having optimal career flow experiences if your primary life role excludes work due to being a full-time student. Regardless of your situation, the good news is that even though optimal career flow tends to happen more in work than in nonwork activities, it can occur in a variety of life roles (student, partner, friend, and so on) *if you are intentional about your behavior*. Additionally, identifying the tasks that connect with optimal career flow for you in the present will help you in your career and educational planning for the future. By identifying those tasks that bring you the most satisfaction, you begin the process of identifying important information to include in your educational and career goals.

## Tip    *Focus on what matters to you.*

When you engage in tasks that matter to you, you feel a greater sense that you matter. So, another question to consider related to optimal career flow is: What matters to you? It is clear that people are more likely to experience optimal career flow when they do work that requires them to use skills they enjoy using and that they feel reasonably competent using. When people engage in activities that allow them to use their skills in these ways, they do not spend much time worrying about whether they will perform competently. When people are not focused on whether they are competent at a particular task, they engage in less inner questioning—e.g., Am I good enough? What if I make a mistake?—and their focus shifts from themselves to the activity. They do not worry so much about *what* they are doing; rather, they focus on doing what they already know they can do. Doing what you like and feel competent doing leads you to experience high levels of satisfaction in your activities.

Because you are more likely to experience optimal career flow when you engage in tasks that reflect what is important to you—or what you value—increasing the probability of your experiencing optimal career flow requires you to be aware of your values as well as your skills. When your activities connect to your values, you do not spend a lot of time pondering the question: *Why* am I doing this? You are in synch with your activities and experience a sense of meaning and purpose in what you are doing. Conversely, when your answers to the question do not reflect your values, you experience inner conflict, which becomes a significant distraction to your capacity to complete the tasks confronting you. When little connection exists between what you do and what you value, you can even become demoralized and depressed. You can easily conclude that what you do does not matter, essentially because it does not matter to you.

When the inevitable challenges arise and you are in a situation that is not consistent with your values, it is very difficult to persevere in that situation. Fortunately, the reverse is also true. When what we do connects with what we value, then it becomes easier to tolerate other challenges in our work situation. Many college students experience this when they compare how they feel in courses that relate to their major versus how they feel when they are enrolled in general education courses that do not connect to their values and interests. In the former, the focus is more likely to be on learning the material being taught. In the latter, the focus is more likely to be on asking the question: "Why do I need to learn this material?" Thus, engaging in activities that reflect our values provides an important source of motivation for most people.

So, to experience optimal career flow in work, it is important, whenever possible, to seek employment opportunities that allow you to do what you enjoy and feel competent doing. When these criteria are met, you are then more likely to experience optimal career flow. You are more likely to find yourself noting that you feel passionate about your work, have an intimate connection with what you do, experience high energy levels, and feel as if time flies by.

## Daryll's Optimal Career Flow

ACTIVITY 8.2

Consider Daryll, from the case example provided at the beginning of the chapter. What do you think is the probability that Daryll will experience optimal career flow in his student teaching experience?

- What factors in Daryll's situation do you think might contribute to his experiencing optimal career flow?

  _____

- What factors do you think might make experiencing optimal career flow less likely to occur for Daryll?

  _____

- What values is Daryll expressing in his student teaching?

  _____

- What skills is he using most often?

  _____

Now consider your own situation by completing the following activity.

## Your Optimal Career Flow

ACTIVITY 8.3

Think of three specific times in your life when you have experienced what you might identify as optimal career flow in your school, leisure, and work activities (try to identify one experience for each activity area). Describe each experience in detail. In your description, address each of the following questions:

**STEP A**

- What were you doing at the time?

  _____

- Who were you with?

  _____

- What was the setting?

  _____

- What happened (before, during, and after)?

  _____

- What were you feeling (physiologically) at the time you had these experiences (describe the physical sensations related to optimal career flow experiences; for example, "I felt lighter, more relaxed, and happy")?

  _____

- What skills were you using?

  _____

- What values were you expressing?

  _____

- What interests were you expressing?

  _____

## STEP B

Take the information identified in Step A and write a one-paragraph statement in which you fill in the blanks below:

In my optimal career flow experiences, I most often use the skills of _____ and express the following values: _____. Other things I notice as important to me in these moments are _____.

## STEP C

Now examine the contexts of your optimal career flow experiences. Identify which activities were solitary activities and which involved others. For the latter:

- Were you working as part of a team?

  _____

- Which type of activity—solitary or group—do you enjoy more?

  _____

- Were you were working indoors or outside?

  _____

_(continued)_

ACTIVITY 8.3
(continued)

- Which do you enjoy more—indoor activities or outside activities?

  _____

- Were you working under time pressure to complete the task or did time not matter? Which do you enjoy more—time pressure or no time pressure—to complete a task?

  _____

Notice anything else that you think is important about your optimal career flow experiences. Describe these.

Now write an overall summary of your optimal career flow experiences including the values, skills, and contexts that tend to be involved in these experiences. To do this, simply complete the following:

- In my optimal career flow experiences, I tend to:

  _____

  _____

  _____

To practice focusing on optimal career flow experiences, over the course of the next two weeks pay attention to when you experience optimal career flow in your leisure activities and in your role as a student, friend, and/or worker. Notice the physical sensations that accompany your optimal career flow experiences. Describe these experiences in a journal. When you have these sensations, make a mental note of what you were doing at the time (better yet, write it down at that point). Keep a journal in which you write daily about your optimal career flow experiences. Describe each moment you had. Reflect (i.e., self-reflection) on what these moments say about you (your feelings, values, motivations, skills, interests, and so on). Then, in a way similar to what you did above, deconstruct what was occurring in those moments and identify the skills, values, interests, and so on that you were expressing at those times. Collectively, these steps help you to develop self-clarity regarding your optimal career flow experiences.

The optimal career flow exercises are important. They are your clues to the sort of activities you may want to engage in more frequently. When you increase your participation in activities that draw on the competencies you enjoy using and that allow you to express your most important values, then you often have reactions similar to those mentioned earlier regarding optimal career flow (e.g., "I feel a sense of passion," "I have a feeling of being in alignment," "I have the sense that this is what life should be about," "I feel natural and genuine"). In other words, you are engaging in the sort of experiences that most likely are desirable and fulfilling for you. These experiences are essential for envisioning your future.

## Visioning

Visioning involves brainstorming future possibilities and identifying desired future scenarios. Put another way, it involves clarifying your dreams for your life and developing your personal vision statement. Focusing on your optimal career flow experiences is an excellent starting point for identifying your desired future possibilities. Creating career opportunities involving your optimal career flow activities maximizes your career satisfaction.

Visioning future possibilities is a creative and fun activity that leads to identifying goals that capture your energy and excitement. Often, however, people need assistance as they create a future vision based on self-clarity. Limiting self-beliefs can often sabotage the process of creating a vision of what your future could be like. Many people think that the future must be like the past, including those things about the past they found unsatisfying. Such people adhere to what psychologists who study optimism refer to as a *fixed mindset*. They believe the past will be the future. They tend to think competencies cannot be improved. They often avoid taking on challenges and tasks because they fear failure. *Fortunately*, everyone fails. We all experience outcomes that we wish were different; however, even these outcomes benefit us. We can learn important lessons from all life experience. The question is how effectively we learn and then use that learning as we move forward.

You may know the story of Michael Jordan, the famous basketball player. As a high school sophomore, Jordan was cut from his high school team. Certainly, this was an outcome he would have preferred not to experience. Jordan could have decided that his ability in basketball was fixed and that he would not be able to improve his skills sufficiently to make his high school varsity basketball team. Rather than using a fixed mindset, however, Jordan had a *growth mindset*. He firmly believed that, through hard work and discipline, he could become a better basketball player. So, rather than becoming a kid who quit playing basketball in his sophomore year of high school because he was not good enough, Jordan went on to become the person many consider to be the best basketball player in history. One of the exciting things about the future is that it has yet to occur!

Future scenarios should be developed free of unnecessary limitations. They should be guided by your self-clarity with minimal input from the *yes, but ...* perspective. To put it another way, future scenarios should not be guided by the reasons you cannot do something. For example, if you love music, are a reasonably accomplished musician, enjoy interacting with other musicians, and find playing music to be especially meaningful, you might envision yourself as a professional musician. The fact that the percentage of musicians who are able to become professional is very small should not, at this point, be considered. Creating as many desirable future scenarios as possible based on your self-clarity should be the goal of visioning.

Consider the following questions: Do you avoid tasks because of fear of failure? Do you put less effort into tasks because you feel hopeless about making progress? Do you miss learning opportunities because of fear of failure? If you answered "yes" to any of these questions, then you probably believe that your potential is fixed. There is, however, hope. Studies have shown that we can change our mindset. To begin this process, you may find it helpful to read about people who have experienced great things. Notice their orientation to thinking about themselves and the future. Consider how you can revise your thinking to increase your orientation to more of a growth mindset.

# Brainstorming Future Possibilities

Developing a growth mindset is critical to successful visioning. In visioning, you use the strategy of brainstorming to identify desired possibilities for your future. Brainstorming involves identifying creative solutions to specific problems or questions. It is something that can be done in groups or individually. Individuals engage in brainstorming to identify a career goal, resolve a relationship issue, make a specific selection from a group of options, and so on.

Specific guidelines are important to follow in order to brainstorm possible career futures effectively. First, brainstorming focuses on quantity—not quality. The goal is to devise a list of career options that is as expansive as possible. No idea is stupid. No idea is bad. Do not take time to engage in self-criticism or dismiss any idea prematurely. Generate as many options as you can. Second, limit the time you set aside for brainstorming. If possible, set a timer. Typically, 10–15 minutes should be sufficient. Whatever timeframe you select, stick to it and make it relatively brief. Limiting your time helps you focus on developing the *quantity* of your list. Third, write down the ideas you generate. You could use sticky notes, for example, and write one idea on each note. See how many sticky notes you can use.

Tip    *In brainstorming, the only bad idea is the one not expressed.*

Begin by reviewing your optimal career flow experiences. Read them over several times, then imagine yourself engaging in several of your optimal career flow experiences one at a time. After you have completed this visualization, complete the following activity.

Once you are done with the activity, take a few moments to notice how you feel and what your energy level is. How do you feel? Are you energized? Because you have been focusing on using your creativity to identify possible futures that

*You must first dream it, then you can achieve it.*

Shutterstock

## Brainstorming Activity

ACTIVITY 8.4

In the next five minutes, complete the sentence below as many times as possible. Write each idea down (ideally on a sticky note). Keep your responses brief. Do not limit yourself to actual jobs. Incorporate as many aspects of yourself as possible. Have some fun, and combine activities into a job you create yourself.

● My dream job is:

incorporate your optimal career flow experiences, there is a good chance that you feel rather positive and energetic right now. Perhaps you are even excited about some of the possibilities you identified. Make a mental note of your reactions. These positive reactions serve as signposts that direct you to activities that will increase your optimal career flow experiences.

Review the possibilities you generated and select three that seem of most interest to you. Examine these possibilities with an eye toward identifying any common themes. For example, Daryll may have themes related to helping children from difficult life circumstances, teaching, organizing, and inspiring others. If so, it might be helpful for him to consider how these themes relate to actual jobs. Once you have identified potential occupations of interest, spend some time learning more about them.

## Personal Vision Statement Guidelines

Using the themes you identified above, you are now ready to develop your *personal vision statement*—a vivid description of your desired future. It is your personal creation of an image that reflects the future you hope to create. It is your dream for yourself. It should be a statement you find compelling and exciting. It should incorporate the most important aspects of who you are, what you enjoy, the skills you enjoy using, and what you value. You are describing the desired destination for your career flow journey. You are creating a statement than can serve as your guide as you make your educational and career plans. It is your opportunity to dream big dreams!

Before writing your vision statement, it is helpful to review some guidelines for this activity. Your vision statement should describe your ideal future career. It should describe the future you hope to create using a future timeframe. Incorporate powerful language to describe a vision that is powerful to you. For example, the vision statement for the organization known as One Laptop Per Child is as follows: "To create educational opportunities for the world's poorest children by providing each child with a rugged, low-cost, low-power, connected laptop with content and software designed for collaborative, joyful, self-empowered learning" (http://laptop.org/en/vision/index. shtml). This is a powerful statement of great ambition. Notice that the creators of this vision statement did not aspire to provide laptops to many middle-class children or even most children living in economically challenged situations. Their vision is much more powerful than that. They seek to provide laptops for all of the poorest children in the world. The statement is compelling and inspirational.

The purpose of your vision statement is to create a mental picture charged with emotion that can serve to energize and inspire you. Take as much space as you need to accomplish this with your vision statement. Be sure to create a vision statement that describes the best possible future outcome for you. Make it just as lofty and ambitious as the vision statement created by those involved in the One Laptop Per Child organization. It should describe what you aspire to achieve. Include as much as you can from your optimal career flow experiences.

It is also important to keep in mind that your vision statement is aspirational. In this sense, it is useful as a guide to assess whether your career is flowing in a direction toward your vision. It is not useful as a measuring stick for assessing whether you have been successful in achieving your vision. For example, the One Laptop Per Child organization will be successful if they significantly increase the number of poor children with laptops living in developing countries. It would not be fair to consider them as unsuccessful if every child does not have a laptop. In this sense, vision statements are idealistic in that they often are nearly impossible to achieve. They are also realistic, however, because they draw on your core values, interests, skills, and future hopes. Thus, they set the course for you to achieve your dreams, and they are a useful tool for stimulating your inspiration, creativity, motivation, and imagination. As Albert Einstein said, "Imagination is more powerful than knowledge." Imagination allows you to see the exciting possibilities for your career. In quoting the Irish playwright, George Bernard Shaw, the late Edward M. Kennedy honored his brother, Robert, by stating that "Some men see things as they are and say, 'Why?' I dream of things that never were and say, 'Why not?'"

### Vision Statement Examples:

I will be a better son, brother, student, teammate, and friend by being reliable, trustworthy, compassionate, and helpful in all my interactions with others.

I will work every summer from now until I graduate from college to save at least $20,000 for graduate school.

I will become an inspirational leader whom people respond to positively because of my vision, creativity, compassion, and excellent work ethic.

I will be a disciplined athlete who consistently goes beyond what my coach expects of me in practice, eat only healthy food, and serve as an excellent role model for all other students.

I will live daily a life dedicated to integrity, commitment, challenge, and joy; be a loving daughter and valued friend; travel the world to experience different cultures; and practice my guitar regularly to become an accomplished guitarist.

## *Your Personal Vision Statement*

ACTIVITY 8.5    Using the activities and guidelines above, construct a vision statement that incorporates what you value the most, what you most enjoy doing, what skills you enjoy using, and what you have always wanted to achieve in your life.

The purpose of the vision statement is to open your eyes to what is possible. It should include what brings you happiness, what you enjoy doing, and what you have always wanted to do. When we become aware of what is possible, we begin to realize that dreams can be achieved and that challenges can be overcome. Review your vision statement regularly, and use it as a stimulus for engaging in self-reflection about whether you are on course in your career and educational planning. You may, on occasion, conclude that you need to revise your vision statement to be more in line with your evolving sense of self.

# Goal Setting

American writer Ralph Waldo Emerson once wrote: "To achieve happiness, we should make certain that we are never without an important goal." Professional basketball player Julius Erving noted: "Goals determine what you're going to be." As these quotes suggest, being without goals is similar to being adrift at sea—subject to the changing tides and currents. Your destination is unclear. When you have goals, you can use them to set your course, guide your activities, and express your purpose. When you engage in self-reflection, develop self-clarity, and use your self-understanding to envision possible future scenarios, you are ready to identify specific goals for your life. As Gloria Steinem, American feminist and author, noted: "Without leaps of imagination, or dreaming, we lose the excitement of possibilities. Dreaming, after all, is a form of planning." When you turn your dreams into vision statements, you establish the foundation for identifying goals and, then, constructing plans to achieve your goals.

Effective goal setting can really only occur after engaging in important foundational work. Hope is essential for developing goals because goals reflect your hope for your future. Goals continue to fuel your hope as you implement plans to move toward the future you hope to achieve. For example, Martin Luther King Jr.'s hope for the future fueled his goal of helping to create a more just society. Hope also boosts your ability to persevere when you encounter obstacles to your goals, and having meaningful goals helps you persevere when your hope needs bolstering. Political/civil activist Jesse Jackson is known for encouraging people to "Keep hope alive!" He knew the necessity for hope when striving toward important goals. Hope is essential for goal identification as well as for implementing your plans to achieve your goals.

Self-reflection and self-clarity are also keys to goal development. When you take time to reflect and become clear about what is important to you, what you enjoy, and what you are good at, then you can use this information to envision the possibilities. In this way, self-clarity becomes your anchor to creating your future vision from which you can develop your personal goals.

# A SMART Goal-Setting Strategy

There are many strategies you can use to identify meaningful career goals. A common and useful strategy is referred to by the acronym SMART. Each letter of the acronym represents an important reminder regarding the goal setting process. The letter "S" refers to the need to make your goals as *specific* as possible. Simply having the goal to lose as much weight as possible, for example, is not sufficient. Having the goal of losing 50 pounds to achieve the weight of 200 pounds from the current weight of 250 pounds is more specific.

Similarly, goals must be *measurable* (the letter "M" in SMART). For example, the goal of working harder at your studies is not as readily measured as a goal that specifies that you will increase your grades from a "C" average to a "B" average.

Goals should also be challenging yet *achievable* (the "A" in SMART). If a goal is viewed as not achievable (and here is where goals differ from vision statements), then you are not likely to work toward it. If a goal is too easy, then you are not likely to be enthusiastic about pursuing that goal. Thus, goals must be challenging enough to energize you but not so challenging that they will lead you to feel hopeless about your chances of achieving them.

Your goals must also be *realistic* (the "R" in SMART), both in terms of what you hope to accomplish and the *timeframe* (the "T" in SMART) in which you hope to accomplish them. If you recently began playing the guitar, for example, to play lead guitar in a touring band within the next six months would not be a very realistic goal. A more realistic goal would be to learn how to strum the basic chords within the next two months.

Note that you should have short-term and long-term goals. Your short-term goals should connect to your long-term goals. For example, a long-term goal could be to lose 50 pounds so that your weight will be 200 pounds from your current weight of 250 pounds, and to achieve this in the next five months. Your short-term goal could be to lose 10 pounds this month so that, by the end of this month, you will weigh 240 pounds. Short-term goals help you to break your long-term goals into relevant, intentional, and achievable "chunks." They help you to keep on course so that your behavior stays focused on achieving your long-term goals.

Setting SMART goals is an evolving process. As you begin working toward your goals, you may need to revise them in several ways. For example, you may realize that they are too easy or too difficult. You may need to adjust your timeframe due to unforeseen events. The point is to revisit your goals as you work toward them to make sure they are still SMART for you! Making sure your goals connect to your vision will help you to stay focused on what it is you desire to achieve. Occasionally, it may be useful to take time to visualize your goal. If your goal is to graduate from college with a degree in architecture, for example, imagine seeing yourself walking across the stage at your graduation ceremony, shaking hands with the dean as she presents your diploma to you. Imagine yourself in your graduation gown and hat and experience all the positive emotions that will accompany this accomplishment. Use this visualization strategy at frequent intervals (it will only take a few minutes, so you may be able to do this three times per week, if not daily). A short-term goal related to your long-term goal could be to increase your study time per day from 30 minutes to 60 minutes six days per week. Be sure to write down your vision statement, long-term goals, and short-term goals. Make sure to reward yourself as you complete your goals!

Tip **If you cannot measure it, you will never know if you have achieved it.**

## SMART Goal Activity

ACTIVITY 8.6    Now, using the information you have acquired about yourself regarding your vision for your future, establish one long-term goal that relates to your vision statement. Make your goal adhere to the SMART criteria. Once you have written your goal, share it with one other person, and tell that person how it meets each SMART criterion.

_____

Now, identify a short-term goal connected to your long-term goal. Make sure this goal also adheres to the SMART criteria.

## Planning

Your short-term goals provide an action plan for you to achieve your long-term goals. The plans you develop to achieve your goals should include key and specific actions you must take, the desired outcomes of these steps, and the timeframe in which they will be completed. Once you have defined a short-term goal using the SMART approach, develop a list of actions you can take to achieve your short-term goal. Identify the information you must acquire, the skills you must use, the behaviors you must demonstrate, and so on to achieve your short-term goal. As you develop your plans to achieve your short-term goals, you will need to prioritize your key action steps. As you complete your short-term goals, make sure to evaluate the information you have acquired and use it to inform your subsequent short-term goals and the plans you develop for each of these.

## Implementing and Adapting

*SMART people make plans to achieve their goals.*

As you implement your plans to achieve your short-term and long-term goals, you will need to monitor and evaluate how effective your plans are in relation to your goals. Pay attention to new information you acquire as you take action. Use new information you learn about yourself and your goals to continually inform your planning steps. If the information you acquire seems to reinforce the plans you are implementing, then that information provides you with important feedback that you are on the correct course to achieve your goals. If the information you acquire seems to indicate that you need to adjust your plans and/or your goals, then it is time to return to the self-reflection and self-clarity steps in the career flow competencies model.

Shutterstock

## *Planning Activity*

ACTIVITY 8.7

To apply the information from this chapter, complete each of the following steps for yourself. Before you do, review each of the steps described in this chapter.

- My Personal Career Vision Statement:

  _____

- My Long-term Career Goal:

  _____

- My Short-term Goal:

  _____

| Key Action Steps | Timeframe | Outcome | Status |
|------------------|-----------|---------|--------|
|                  |           |         |        |
|                  |           |         |        |
|                  |           |         |        |

As you implement your plans and take actions toward achieving your goals, reflect on what you are learning about yourself and your goals. What do you know now that you did not know when you first implemented your plans to achieve your goals? What does this new knowledge suggest relative to whether you should revise either your plans and/or your goals? Be careful not to judge any needed revision as negative. It is, in fact, just the opposite. Using new information appropriately is very wise. If you consider the fact that you are always acquiring new information about yourself and your situation, then it would be silly not to take full advantage of this new information as you manage your career flow. Being personally flexible in this way will help increase the probability that you will achieve a goal that you find desirable and fulfilling.

## Summary

People desire work experiences that they find meaningful and enjoyable. Although these experiences are not likely to describe anyone's total work experience, they are essential for satisfying work activity. By focusing on the tasks that are important to you and the skills that you enjoy using, you are able to identify the activities most likely to result in optimal career flow experiences.

Daryll seems well positioned in his student teaching experience to have optimal career flow experiences. He has achieved this position in his career by focusing on his values and what he enjoys doing—by focusing on what matters to him. By focusing on what matters to you, you can achieve the same position in your career and increase the probability of having optimal career flow experiences.

Identifying long-term and short-term goals as well as plans to achieve your goals are important steps in the career flow process. Although these steps are grounded in information you have gathered about yourself and your potential options, there is always a bit of a gap between the information you have before you take action and the information you acquire as you take steps toward achieving your goals. The new information you acquire as you move toward your goals can be used to inform you as to whether the action steps you are taking are directing you toward the destination you truly desire. When necessary, make the adjustments you need to make to your goals and/or plans. You will repeat these steps many times over the course of your career as you move toward destinations you desire.

## Questions for Reflection and Discussion

1. Review Daryll's story. How did he incorporate his experiences as a child into his current goals? How might you do the same? Try to identify what mattered most to you when you were young. How might that be important to you in your future?

2. Read an autobiography of someone whom you admire. Try to identify whether this person experienced optimal career flow in his or her work. If so, what did she or he use consistent pronouns (this person, they, he or she) do to achieve optimal career flow? What can you learn about optimal career flow from your subject's experiences?

3. Identify a time when you had to revise your goals. How did you make the decision to revise your goals? What information helped you decide that it was time to revise your goals?

4. What do you think are the most important things to consider in setting a goal?

5. How would you assess whether a goal is a good goal or a poorly formed goal?

## References and Resources

Mihaly Csikszentmihalyi: Creativity, fulfillment and flow at YouTube; presentation at the February, 2004 TED conference.

A brief description of "flow": http://coe.sdsu.edu/eet/articles/Flowexp/start.htm

Reading materials related to flow:
Csikszentmihalyi, Mihaly (1988). *Optimal Experience: Psychological Studies of Flow in Consciousness.* Cambridge, NY: Cambridge University Press. 323.

Csikszentmihalyi, Mihaly (1990). *Flow: The Psychology of Optimal Experience.* New York: Harper and Row.

The following websites provide more information about SMART goals: www.mindtools.com/pages/article/newHTE_87.htm

http://ezinearticles.com/?Five-Basics-of-the-Goal-Setting-Theory&id=2469149

> " If you can't explain it simply, you don't understand it well enough. "
>
> —*Albert Einstein*

# 9

# Connecting to the World of Work: Research, Job Leads, and Trend-Spotting

## OBJECTIVES

This chapter focuses on the important topic of world-of-work information and how to use this information in your career planning. After reading this chapter, you will be able to:

- Conduct occupational research to discover background and emerging trends
  - Use observations and people within your network as sources of career information
  - Conduct culture audits
  - Engage in job shadowing or work experiences to find out more about specific careers

- Find a career focus through integrating self-assessment results and workplace information

- Clearly communicate your career goals using "elevator statements"

- Identify sources of specific job leads, including those within the "hidden" job market

- Continue to spot trends that will impact your career

## CASE STUDY

Nick was about to graduate. For four years, he had maintained a long-distance relationship with his fiancée, Corinne; while Nick was at school, Corinne had remained living in the rural community they both grew up in. Nick and Corinne

istockphoto

135

were excited about finally getting married this summer. They had agreed to live in a home on Corinne's family farm to help care for Corinne's grandparents. Corinne had taken on increasing eldercare responsibilities after her mother died two years ago. Her grandmother was less able to care for her husband (Corinne's grandfather) after his recent stroke but, with Corinne's physical help and Corinne's father's financial support, they were able to continue to live together on the farm.

Nick is equally committed to caring for extended family—he is happy to support Corinne financially so that she can work reduced hours and care for her grandparents. He is familiar with this way of life and it suits his personal values and preferences. Nick grew up on a neighboring farm under similar circumstances, with his mother and aunt caring for their elderly parents and his father taking on management of the family farm. He loves Corinne, her family, their church, and their beautiful rural community nestled in a valley between two mountains. He can't imagine a better place to raise the children they hope to have; Nick and Corinne both hope they can afford for Corinne to stay home full time while their children are young.

One significant difference between Nick and his dad and future father-in-law, however, is that Nick doesn't intend to work on the farm. Both his and Corinne's fathers are relatively young—neither expects to retire for another 20–25 years. Nick has been studying business at school; neither of the family businesses is large enough to need a full-time manager or to pay a sufficient salary. The economy in their rural community is not thriving; like Nick, most of his friends left home after graduation. Unlike Nick, most aren't planning to come back except for Christmas and major family events. The nearest city is a 90-minute drive away. Nick's preference is definitely not to commute for 3 hours each day if he can find work closer to home.

Although Nick has compelling reasons to look for work locally, almost all job seekers have a preferred place to work. This chapter will equip you to identify job possibilities that are a good personal fit and realistic within your regional economy. You will learn about sources of information for diverse occupations, techniques for gathering firsthand information about various sectors and organizations, and tips for networking effectively to generate specific job leads. All of these pieces are important as you finalize your career planning and prepare to move into the implementation stage of the career flow model.

## Conduct Occupational Research: Background and Emerging Trends

As you begin to actively search for work, there are many layers of information to consider. The career flow model highlights the importance of ongoing self-reflection, self-clarity, visioning, goal setting, and planning. To prepare to move into the implementing and adapting stages of career flow, it is essential to gather current information about occupations, organizations, and industries or sectors you are considering to ensure your career goals are viable in the present economy.

For general descriptions of almost 1,000 different occupations, visit the O*Net Dictionary of Occupational Titles at www.dictionary-occupationaltitles.net/. For each occupation, read a brief description of tasks, relevant tools and technology, knowledge, skills, abilities, work activities, work context, job zone (i.e., qualifications/ preparation), interests, work styles, work values, wages, and employment trends, as well as links to information about related occupations. Drilling deeper into the O*Net resources, you can find regionally specific content.

Surfing the Internet and browsing through local and national newspapers can provide more current information about workplace realities; corporate websites and annual reports, professional associations, and sector or industry councils often offer very specific, timely, and relevant insights. Use your O*Net research as a good starting place from which to further explore changes in the dynamic world of work. For example, due to the impending retirement of countless baby boomers, skill shortages are anticipated within many organizations and across industry sectors and occupational groups. However, global shifts in supply and demand impact such projections—for example, the huge shifts in the U.S. automotive industry experienced in 2009—therefore, it is essential to access current news sources before finalizing your career goals.

## Occupational Highlights and Current Trends

**ACTIVITY 9.1**

To practice, select two occupational titles to explore. Use the table below to anchor key points from the O*Net Dictionary of Occupational Titles. Then, for each occupation, access at least three current sources of information (i.e., information published within the past three months). Note any information that confirms or contradicts your O*Net results.

| Occupation | O*Net Highlights | Recent Updates (Indicate source and date published) |
|---|---|---|
|  |  |  |
|  |  |  |
|  |  |  |

Shutterstock

*Conduct informational interviews to learn about workplace trends or organizational culture.*

## Use Observations and Networks as Sources of Career Information

Once you have gathered and critiqued as much information as possible using print and Internet resources, it is important to confirm your findings with people who are actively engaged in the field or organization you are investigating. This is commonly known as *informational interviewing*.[1]

Your *network* is in simplest terms the group of people you interact with; it may include family, friends, other students, coworkers at your part-time job, teammates on your soccer team, or friends of friends. As you begin gathering career information (and later, specific job leads), it may be helpful to begin to organize the contact information of these important people into your address book or database.

You may already have people in your personal or professional network who are well positioned to provide you with up-to-date, relevant information. If not, approach people in your network to see if they may know someone who knows someone who can answer your questions. Warm calls are generally easier to make than cold calls; therefore, beginning with people you know and using their names to open doors with the next level of contacts can make your research process go much more smoothly. Don't overlook the power of social networking through online groups; Facebook, LinkedIn, and similar sites can quickly expand your network and introduce you to relevant contacts in the industry, occupations, or geographic regions that interest you.

## Informational Interviewing

ACTIVITY 9.2

To practice informational interviewing, begin by asking at least three of your contacts about the two occupations you researched in the previous activity. In the table provided, write down any relevant new information you gather. For example, Nick asked both his dad and future father-in-law about businesses in their community that seemed to be growing or where managers were due to retire soon.

[1] For tips on the kinds of questions to ask during an informational interview, go to: http://www.quintcareers.com/information_interview.html

| Occupation | People I Contacted/ When? | Current Information |
|---|---|---|
| Manager | Dad<br>Corinne's Dad | There's a new hardware store opening up; Co-op store feed department manager is retiring in September. |
| | | |
| | | |
| | | |

## Conduct Culture Audits

Aside from the objective and factual information you access through print and Internet sources and personal contacts, there is a subjective side to the job search. You are looking for an organization that "fits." Similarly, hiring managers are looking for employees who fit within their organizational culture.

 Tip *The culture of an organization is like its personality; essentially, it's the blueprint for how things get done.*

Values, beliefs, attitudes, and behaviors all contribute to organizational culture. Culture impacts interactions among customers, employees, and management as well as the kinds of results that are rewarded within the organization.

Conduct *culture audits* to identify some of the subtle indicators of what it will be like to work within industries and organizations you are seriously considering. Identify aspects of organizational culture that are relevant to you; this informs your self-clarity in the career flow model. Clues may include visible artifacts (e.g., the location and type of building, how people dress, whether or not workers look happy, indications of onsite daycare or fitness facilities, public signage or sponsorships, recruitment packages that describe benefits or support for education). Also, listen for conversational clues such as whether employees and managers interact with respect, evidence of positioning within the industry, and a sense of hope and engagement or being stuck.

## Culture Audit

ACTIVITY 9.3

To conduct a culture audit, first identify the specific types of information you hope to collect (e.g., how women are treated in the industry; whether the organization is "family friendly"; how long it generally takes for people to get promoted; whether most employees stay with the organization for more than two years). Next, identify the best source for each type of information; for example, does the organization's website provide any clues? Is there public access to observing the workplace, as in the front end of a community agency or public utility company? Do workers tend to leave the building at specific times of day and line up for public transit? Do they eat in local restaurants? Select one organization to audit. Use the table provided below to record your findings. Nick chose to visit the co-op store when he was home for the weekend; he was particularly interested in whether it seemed like a place where younger people enjoyed working.

| Type of Information | Potential Source | Cultural Findings |
|---|---|---|
| Do younger people like working here? | In-store observation; neighbor who works there | High energy and laughter; employees have curling and softball teams; people don't quit |
| | | |
| | | |
| | | |
| | | |
| | | |
| | | |

You can likely collect most of your information through passive observation rather than direct contact. However, you may find it helpful to access a "cultural informant." Similar to an informational interview, this informant can help you to understand how the industry or organization operates. Use your network to identify a cultural informant, just as you did for other informational interviews. Questions for a cultural informant may include:

What's great about working here? What's not?

Who fits in? Who doesn't? Why not? What happens when people don't fit?

What kinds of things are taken really seriously here? Why?

## Engage in Job Shadowing or Work Experiences

For the next level of information gathering, it may be helpful to arrange an in-person observation. As discussed in the previous section about culture audits, it's possible to observe some workplaces without making any special arrangements.

Tip   *Whenever you are shopping, using public transit, or accessing a service within your own community, take the opportunity to watch others work. Notice both attitudes and actions. (Do the workers seem happy? Engaged? Frustrated? Bored?) Consider what appeals to you about the jobs you observe every day. What doesn't? Why?*

At this point, your career goals likely aren't completely random. Therefore, now is a good time to arrange to "job shadow" someone in an occupation or specific organization that interests you. If you have access to a job shadowing or work experience program at school, take advantage of it.

Tip   *Job shadowing provides a unique opportunity for an insider's look at an occupation.*

If you don't have access to a formal program, use your network to identify someone to shadow. Some organizations will have security concerns (e.g., individuals may need security clearance before being permitted onsite). In such cases, getting a police check and signing a confidentiality agreement may be all it takes to get permission to shadow. It can be well worth the effort; job shadowing provides a unique opportunity to see the day-to-day operations of an occupation, industry, or organization you are seriously considering.

Work experiences, whether volunteer, program-related (e.g., practica, co-op placements, internships, or apprenticeships), or part-time or seasonal employment, can also be useful ways to research career possibilities. Similar to job shadowing, work experiences provide an insider's look at a variety of occupations within an organization and industry. However, work experiences go far beyond job shadowing, as you get the opportunity to contribute your skills, develop new ones, build professional relationships, and check out "fit." Take advantage of any work experience opportunities available; they will all help to inform your specific career goals and plans.

To fully benefit from job shadowing or work experiences, prepare in advance. Identify specific questions or learning goals. While onsite, look for opportunities to demonstrate your knowledge and skills. Where appropriate, offer immediate assistance or do some quick research to help solve problems you observe. Finally, strengthen professional relationships by following up after your job shadow or work experience opportunity.

## Find a Career Focus: Integrate Self-Assessment Results and Workplace Information

The career flow model begins with self-reflection, self-clarity, and goal setting. Through activities in this chapter, you've accumulated valuable information about occupations, industries, and specific organizations that interest you. The next step is a crucial one, as you integrate all of this information to find a viable career focus (i.e., work you'd like to do and that needs doing).

## Career Options

ACTIVITY 9.4        Use the table below to systematically compare the specific career options you are
considering to highlights from your self-assessments and career research. Nick, for
example, is focused on finding a management position as close to his small rural
community as possible.

| Occupation | Self-Assessments | Career Research | Notes/Next Steps |
|---|---|---|---|
| Manager | Theme: Excellent leadership skills; highly organized | General and operations managers are in-demand occupations | Talk to network contacts in community; follow-up on leads for co-op manager and new hardware store |
| | | | |
| | | | |
| | | | |

As you reflect on your findings, keep in mind that your career goals will continue to evolve for the rest of your life. At this stage, you are simply looking for sufficient focus to generate specific job leads. Eventually, you will outgrow any job that may suit you perfectly right now. In some cases, you can enrich your career within the same occupation, sector, or organization. However, in other cases, you'll need to reposition your career to re-establish career flow. As your personal career journey continues, ongoing self-reflection will lead to enhanced self-clarity, new visions, and adjusted goals and plans. As a result, you'll adapt to personal and contextual changes and strategically implement new career strategies. The career flow cycle is continuous.

The next sections of this chapter, however, equip you to implement the goals that you are currently focused on. A helpful first step will be to develop a short statement that clearly communicates your career goal. These are commonly called *elevator statements* or *30-second commercials*.

## Communicate Career Goals Using Elevator Statements

It is important to be able to clearly communicate your career goals, so that others in your network understand exactly what you are looking for and will be able to help you generate work opportunities. Elevator statements derive their name from those brief chance encounters that may open future doors; consider Nick finding himself in an elevator with the soon-to-be-retiring manager at the co-op store. What can he say to indicate interest in, and knowledge about, the organization? How can he wisely invest 30 seconds to generate interest in a follow-up meeting?

Important chance encounters happen anywhere, of course, not just in elevators. Consider the countless people you run into in your day-to-day activities (e.g., getting a coffee between classes, at a friend's house for dinner, at the grocery store, or while getting a haircut). We've previously discussed the importance of happenstance or serendipity. Your elevator statement equips you to capitalize on happenstance; don't let great opportunities slip away because you didn't know what to say.

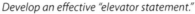

*Develop an effective "elevator statement."*

istockphoto

## *Elevator Statement*

**ACTIVITY 9.5**    Use the space below to craft an elevator statement. Be sure it contains two types of information: (1) your career goal(s) or specific job focus and (2) how your qualifications support that goal. Create several statements if you are still exploring more than one career option. Be creative; make sure your elevator statement is memorable and compelling. (See Vessenes (2009) in the Additional Resources section at the end of this chapter for a step-by-step process for getting started.) Nick's statement, to be used with local businesses, is: "Hi, I'm Nick Baerg—Tim Baerg's son. I've been at college for the past four years, but I'm getting married and moving back as soon as I graduate in May. I'm looking for a management position in a small business or another role that will use some of my business training. I have a business degree and seven years of experience in part-time summer jobs in the offices of a variety of local businesses, and over twenty years of experience on the farm. I also know almost everyone in the area—my family has farmed here for over a hundred years."

| Elevator Statement |
| --- |
| My goal: |
| My qualifications: |

## Identify Sources of Specific Job Leads

You are now nearing the implementation stage of career flow; with plans in place, you are ready to generate specific job leads. You're likely already aware of good sources for advertised jobs (e.g., career services within your college, online job boards,[1] newspapers, career pages on organizations' websites, and so on). Professional associations and unions may also provide job leads. Many employers use generic resources such as Craig's List (www.craigslist.com) to advertise jobs as well as their products and services. It's important to check all of these sources for jobs that might interest you and fit with your qualifications.

You may not realize that the vast majority of jobs are never advertised; estimates range as high as 90–95 percent, depending on the industry and local economy. To access these hidden jobs, your network will be invaluable; that's one of the reasons your elevator statement is so important. People who know you need to know exactly

[1]See the Appendix at the end of this chapter for links to a selection of online job boards.

## *Exploring Advertised Jobs*

ACTIVITY 9.6

Use the table below to list 5–10 sources of advertised jobs within the industries you are exploring.

| # | Advertised Jobs within the Industry You Are Exploring |
|---|---|
| 1 | |
| 2 | |
| 3 | |
| 4 | |
| 5 | |
| 6 | |
| 7 | |
| 8 | |
| 9 | |
| 10 | |

what you're looking for and how you are qualified for that kind of work; otherwise, they won't recognize the perfect opportunity for you when they hear about it.

Generally, unadvertised jobs cluster into three categories. In some cases, a job is specifically created to suit you because you have made a great impression on a potential employer. This often happens following practicum or work experience placements; after employers have invested several weeks or months in training, they usually don't want to lose a good employee. If at all possible, many will cobble together a job to keep you on the team. Sometimes informational interviews result in unsolicited job offers; these types of jobs also fit within this category.

The second type of unadvertised job is when there is a clear need but nobody has taken the time to advertise it, perhaps because there is no time or human resource capacity to engage in a sophisticated hiring process. In such cases, managers may ask friends, colleagues, employees, or customers for referrals. This is where members of your network can be particularly helpful, sharing relevant leads they hear about. Ask them to tell you about upcoming parental leaves, sabbaticals, or openings due to employees leaving for school, retirement, or other opportunities. Also, ask them to monitor extended health leaves, new projects, or seasonal surges in business.

The third type of unadvertised job is an internal posting. In such cases, the job has technically been advertised, but only to a select group of people. However, if someone shares such a posting with you, don't hesitate to apply. In many organizations, especially governments and those with unions, it is important to find out if an internal candidate is qualified or interested. However, once internal candidates have been exhausted, the next step is generally to open the search to external candidates. If you learned of the job before it was publicly posted, your application may result in a hiring decision before others even know the job was available.

## *Unadvertised Jobs*

ACTIVITY 9.7     Use the table below to identify 10 potential sources of unadvertised jobs within your industry or sector.

| # | Unadvertised Jobs Within Your Industry or Sector |
|---|---|
| 1 | |
| 2 | |
| 3 | |
| 4 | |
| 5 | |
| 6 | |
| 7 | |
| 8 | |
| 9 | |
| 10 | |

There are many effective strategies for generating specific job leads. Stay actively connected to the world of work through:

- networking events, volunteer experiences, and work placements;
- warm and, if necessary, cold calls where you actively express your interest in a specific occupation, sector, or industry; and
- continuing to monitor publicly advertised openings.

## Spot Trends That Will Impact Your Career

Your career research needs to continue long after you land the job of your dreams. As technology continues to change how we work, global economies become increasingly interconnected, and new occupations appear that didn't exist when you began your job search, it's important to monitor those changes and reflect on how they may impact your career. This fits with the adapting stage of career flow, where you evaluate information that is constantly changing, respond to it proactively, and re-enter the self-reflection stage to begin the cycle once again.

## *Changes in Technology*

ACTIVITY 9.8     Use the table provided to consider how changes in technology may impact your career and how you can effectively respond. For example, Nick realizes that managers increasingly need to be comfortable using web-based databases, documents, and communication tools.

| Changes in Technology | Impact on Your Career | Your Response to These Changes |
|---|---|---|
| Web-based tools | Rural managers are instantly connected to head office and central databases and inventory tracking systems | Completed 3 elective courses in emerging technologies for net-worked organizations |
| | | |
| | | |
| | | |
| | | |

Some trends are related to global economies; others are industry, occupation, or organization specific. For example, when one local business shuts down, another related business may offer expanded services to fill the gap. When new standards are introduced within an industry, some occupational groups will be privileged while other workers lose their jobs.

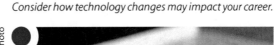

*Consider how technology changes may impact your career.*

istockphoto

## Five Trends

ACTIVITY 9.9    Revisit your career research. Use the table below to list five trends that are presently impacting work within your chosen occupation, sector, or geographic region. Nick's research indicates an increasing demand for managers. He also realizes that technology means more office duties can be managed from a centralized location.

| # | 5 Trends Impacting Your Work |
|---|---|
| **e.g.** | Up to 2016, 441,00 additional employees are expected to be needed to fill general and operation managers positions (http://online.onetcenter.org/link/summary/11-1021.00). |
| **1** | |
| **2** | |
| **3** | |
| **4** | |
| **5** | |

The ways people work continue to change as well. As you monitor relevant trends, consider whether most of the work in your sector is project-driven or permanent full-time. Are workers typically self-employed, contractors, or employees? Where do people generally work? From home? Local offices? Centralized headquarters? Are any jobs outsourced to workers from other countries?

## Logistics of Work

ACTIVITY 9.10    Use the following table to record your findings about the logistics of work within the occupation, sector, or geographic regions you are exploring. For example, Nick found that management positions are generally full-time but consulting positions are project-based.

| Characteristic | Occupation: _____ | Occupation: _____ |
|---|---|---|
| Project vs. Permanent | | |
| Part-time vs. Full-time | | |
| Self-Employed, Contract, Employee | | |

| Location: Home, Local, Head Office, International | | |
|---|---|---|
| Other (list characteristics) | | |
| | | |
| | | |

Trend-spotting can help you to predict types of work that may be potentially more stable. Generally, capitalizing on several trends concurrently will maximize your employment security. For example, in a knowledge-based economy, with an increasingly diverse workforce and a rapidly aging population, it makes sense that a well-educated, multilingual, culturally competent health services manager would be in high demand.

## Impact of Trends on Careers

ACTIVITY 9.11    Use the table below to list three careers you are exploring, identify three to five relevant trends impacting each, and evaluate the impact of those trends on demand for those specific careers. For example, Nick realizes that, due to a trend toward centralized computerized management systems, some management positions will likely be based in the city.

| Career | Trends | Impact |
|---|---|---|
| Accounting Manager | Centralized accounting system | Limited opportunities in large organizations in rural location |
| | | |
| | | |
| | | |
| | | |
| | | |

Have you considered an international/global career? As the Internet provides access to career information from all around the world, it has become increasingly easy to monitor and respond to economic trends in other regions. Even if you choose not to leave home, you are likely to be impacted by the global economy or

# *Impact of the Global Economy*

ACTIVITY 9.12    Use the space below to describe the potential impact of the global economy on the careers you are considering. As Nick reflected on this, he realized that technology could allow him to do work from home—it wouldn't matter where he lived. He started to research multinational firms that did business with local farmers.

| Career | Global Trends | Potential Impact |
|---|---|---|
| Account Manager | Growth of small and home-based businesses; trend toward large multinational suppliers | Consider starting a home-based business as a local account manager for several large suppliers |
| | | |
| | | |

may work within a multinational organization with colleagues from diverse corners of the world; it is therefore important to understand how the global economy may affect your own career.

## Summary

Nick, from the case example at the beginning of this chapter, has almost finished his business degree. He is hopeful that he can find a job in the rural community where he and his fiancée, Corinne, grew up and where Corinne is currently caring for older members of her family. As hope is the center of the career flow model, it is important that Nick's hope be sustained. To do this, hope will need to interact with each of the other elements of the model.

To begin his search for work, Nick engaged in some self-reflection. He recognized that he didn't want to be a farmer like his father and father-in-law. He examined his personal circumstances, acknowledging that he was ready to begin to build a home and a family with Corinne. He realized that his values and preferences suited returning to his small rural community; he believed that, despite the changes in the local economy, it was the place he wanted to raise their future children.

Nick's reflections led to some self-clarity. He knew where he wanted to live and work, and why (i.e., subjective self-clarity from the career flow model). However, he also recognized the objective reality that there were limited opportunities for full-time work for a business manager in his struggling rural community; he knew that he didn't want to do a daily 3-hour commute. Nick's reflections and discussions with Corinne and his family also resulted in life role clarity; he valued Corinne's commitment to caring for her extended family and he wanted to be able to financially support her to do that. Although he didn't want to work as a farmer, he was happy to live on the farm and play an active role in his church and community.

In the following questions for discussion and reflection, you will have an opportunity to apply the rest of the career flow model to Nick's situation, helping with visioning through brainstorming future possibilities, then setting some short- and longer-term goals with plans for how to achieve them. Finally, you will grapple with how Nick could implement the plans you envision. How will he measure success? What personal flexibility will he need to draw on to experience a satisfying career flow?

This chapter focused on supplementing your visioning and goal-setting activities through investigating the realities of the workplace you will enter. You have learned how to find background information about occupations, industries, and specific organizations that interest you. Besides accessing print and Internet-based information, you have learned about the importance of informational interviewing, culture audits, and experiential activities to explore the current realities of work and workplaces you are considering. Many of the activities in this chapter were designed to help you integrate what you know about yourself—the self-reflection, self-clarity, visioning, and goal-setting aspects of the career flow model—with information you were able to uncover about current trends in specific careers. You learned how to create elevator statements so that you will be prepared to talk clearly about your career goals and qualifications. You also learned about generating specific job leads, including those in the hidden job market (i.e., unadvertised work opportunities). The chapter ended with a reminder that trend-spotting needs to be a lifelong activity as you continue your career journey. The workplace will continue to evolve and, just as you have to monitor changes in the water as you paddle down a river, you need to stay alert to changes in regional and global economies that may impact your career. This chapter concludes the visioning, goal-setting, and planning components of career flow; you are now ready to focus on strategies for implementing and adapting your career goals.

## Questions for Reflection and Discussion

1. Nick, our case example for this chapter, is almost finished with his business degree and ready to find a job. Take a moment to reread the case description (from the beginning of the chapter and the conclusion) and note all important considerations that impact Nick's career. In groups of three, brainstorm some career possibilities that Nick could consider. Be creative—the best solution for Nick may not be a traditional full-time job. Engage in some trend-spotting. How has farm management changed in recent years? How has technology helped individuals avoid or minimize long commutes? Agree on a short- and long-term goal for Nick, supporting both with clear and realistic plans for achieving them. Finally, identify practical steps Nick can take for connecting with his future employer(s). How will personal flexibility help him to achieve career success that is fulfilling, meets his financial needs, and serves his community?

2. With a partner, conduct a culture audit of your current school or a local business. What visible artifacts give you tangible clues about what it might be

like to work there? What questions do you have that you can't easily find answers to? Who might be a good cultural informant? How could you contact him or her?

3. With a partner, work on your elevator statements. Can you each say them in 30 seconds or less? Provide concrete feedback—as an outsider, would you understand enough about your partner's job of interest that you would recognize an opportunity if you stumbled across it? Were you convinced that your partner was qualified (i.e., would you pass on a good lead)?

## Additional Resources

National Center for O*NET Development. (n.d.). *O*NET online*. Retrieved July 29, 2009, from http://online.onetcenter.org/. The O*NET website is a prime source for US career information. The O*NET database contains information on hundreds of jobs and is free to all users. Individuals can use this site to search jobs, use career exploration tools, and take self-assessments.

Quintessential Careers. (n.d.). *Informational interviewing tutorial*. Retrieved July 29, 2009, from http://www.quintcareers.com/information_interview.html. Being prepared for an informational interview is just as important as being prepared for a job interview. That's why knowing what questions to ask during an informational interview and preparing them in advance is crucial. This resource provides some basic informational interview questions to ask and provides a link to more than 200 more questions.

Vessenes, K. (2009). *Five steps to creating your elevator statement*. Retrieved July 29, 2009, from http://www.producersweb.com/r/VA/d/contentFocus/?adcID= 10f0009d1cd62ca63c9838df541c994d. This is a great resource for creating a punchy elevator statement in five simple steps. This resource is complete with an elevator statement template provided in step 3 and sample statements.

## Appendix: Online Sources of Advertised Jobs

America's Job Bank—www.jobbankinfo.org/
- Although America's job bank ended operations in July 2007, you can access specific state job banks online
- Use this link to your local job bank

America's Job Exchange—www.americasjobexchange.com/
- Post your resume and browse through job postings
- Access career centers and resources

CareerJet—www.careerjet.com/
- Search jobs by industry or location

JobBankUSA—www.jobbankusa.com/
- Post your resume, search jobs, and access valuable job seeker resources; obtain educational information in the education center

Monster—www.monster.com/
- Create a profile, post your resume/cover letter, and/or search through job listings
- Access career tools and advice

USA Jobs—http://jobsearch.usajobs.gov/
- Search for jobs and access the information center
- Resume builder available

"The pessimist complains about the wind; the optimist expects it to change; the realist adjusts the sails."
—William A. Ward

# CHAPTER 10

# Turning Possibilities into Realities

## OBJECTIVES

This chapter focuses on important job search topics such as resume writing, compiling a career portfolio, and managing references effectively. After reading this chapter, you will be able to:

- Customize resumes and cover letters

- Write more effectively

- Compile a career portfolio

- Manage the impression you create

- Manage references who will confirm your qualifications

## CASE STUDY

Jon Hiroto always struggles to answer the question, "Where are you from?" Jon has a European Union (EU) passport, identifying him as a British citizen; his mom is British and she returned "home" to be close to her mother for the months just before and after Jon was born. His father is American; his grandfather on his Dad's side was born in Japan and Jon looks quite a bit like him. But, other than the month after he was born and brief visits during school vacations, Jon had never lived in Britain, Japan, or the United States until he was accepted at an American university for his degree in international development. His accent is an unusual mixture of British and American; in combination with his slightly Asian appearance and his Japanese last name, others are curious about his background and tend to ask, "So ... where are you from?"

Shutterstock

155

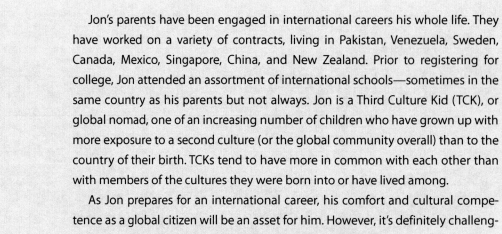

Jon's parents have been engaged in international careers his whole life. They have worked on a variety of contracts, living in Pakistan, Venezuela, Sweden, Canada, Mexico, Singapore, China, and New Zealand. Prior to registering for college, Jon attended an assortment of international schools—sometimes in the same country as his parents but not always. Jon is a Third Culture Kid (TCK), or global nomad, one of an increasing number of children who have grown up with more exposure to a second culture (or the global community overall) than to the country of their birth. TCKs tend to have more in common with each other than with members of the cultures they were born into or have lived among.

As Jon prepares for an international career, his comfort and cultural competence as a global citizen will be an asset for him. However, it's definitely challenging trying to explain his nomadic existence to potential employers. Sometimes he wishes there were an easier answer to what others seem to think is simply small talk: "Where are you from?"

Jon's international background makes writing a resume challenging as well. He wonders how to adequately portray his diverse experiences, especially within only a couple of pages. Jon's other issue is that he has absolutely no paid work experience. Jon's school vacations were the only time his parents could take him "home" to their own countries to spend time with friends and family and, because Jon was generally at boarding school, his family also used their vacation time to explore their current region together. As a result, unlike many other students, Jon had never worked during school vacations.

Jon is a bit worried about his transition from school to work. He knows he has much to offer potential employers, especially in international settings. However, he finds the practicalities of communicating those assets quite daunting. Similarly, but perhaps for quite different reasons, you might be a bit concerned about how to clearly communicate your qualifications for the career you hope to enter.

Hope is the center of the career flow model, and it interacts with each of the essential competencies: self-reflection; self-clarity; visioning, goal setting, and planning; and implementing and adapting. As you work through this chapter, you will need to use each of these career flow competencies as you begin to implement and adapt your job search plans. Through engaging in practical activities, constructing customized documents, and strategically managing the impression you intend to portray, you will likely experience a renewed hopefulness about securing work that fits you well.

Although your story is likely quite different from Jon's, we all share the challenge of trying to adequately convey our life experiences within a short resume and cover letter. Increasingly, career experts are also recommending that individuals create career portfolios to showcase their skills. Defining your personal "brand" and managing the impressions others will form of you, both in person and online, are essential to your job search success. Another important asset to support your job search will be excellent references; it's important to coach your references so they can speak effectively about your relevant strengths. All of these important components of turning career possibilities into realities are discussed in this chapter.

# Resumes and Cover Letters

Almost everyone will be asked for a resume at some point in their career. Whether it's to support the co-op office in coordinating work term placements, to leave with a recruiter at a career fair to indicate your interest in his or her company, to justify your request for a raise or promotion within your current organization, or to give to a friend who has heard of some openings at work, it's important to have an up-to-date resume on hand that can be quickly targeted for opportunities that arise. In the following sections, we will introduce two distinct purposes for your resume, four common resume styles, and several resume formats. Although most people would like a resume template to follow, our belief is that the best approach to developing your resume is to customize it for your unique purposes.

## Resume Purposes

There are two primary purposes for a resume, and each purpose requires a slightly different format. First, a resume is useful as an ongoing inventory of all of your work, education, and relevant life experiences. For this purpose, keep a master resume. Your master resume can be as long as it needs to be; it is never going to leave your computer. The sole purpose of a master resume is to keep track of your work and educational history, including relevant contact information, dates, job titles, courses, memberships, and accomplishments. Do not worry about formatting this version; just keep adding things as you think of them, ideally in reverse-chronological order (i.e., most recent first).

Tip    *In essence, the master resume is the unedited history of your life as it relates to your career.*

The second purpose for a resume, however, is as a sales tool. For this purpose, your resume must be targeted and persuasive. It will be used to convince recruiters or hiring managers that you have what they are looking for, that you are worth considering for an interview.

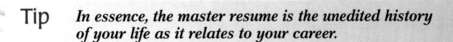

## *Creating a Targeted Resume*

ACTIVITY 10.1    To create a targeted resume, follow these simple steps:

1. Open your master resume.

2. Save it with a new file name, specific to the job you are looking for (e.g., your name_company_year_month_date). This ensures that you won't unintentionally submit a resume that was targeted for a different position.

3. Carefully check your contact information and adjust if necessary.
   a. If you are applying to a job that isn't local, consider providing a local address (e.g., a relative's) if possible, to indicate a connection to that region; some

*(continued)*

employers are reluctant to consider someone from out of the area, worried that there may be travel costs for interviews or relocation. If you don't have a local connection, consider using your cover letter to mention your interest in the region, your plans for relocating, or your willingness to travel to interviews at your own expense.

b. Make sure your email address is appropriate for professional use. For example, make sure it doesn't read chocoholic@x.com but, rather, jsmith@x.com.

c. If providing your cell phone number, be sure to answer professionally.

d. If providing a home number, ensure that the voicemail is appropriate and that everyone answering the phone knows that you are applying for work.

e. Some immigrants and international students use an English name as well as the official name on their transcripts and legal documents. If you choose to do this, make sure that those answering your phone know the other names you are using; also be sure to have some documentation clearly linking both names to you!

4. Apply the "Who cares?" filter to your master resume.

a. With the job you are applying for in mind, go through your master resume (the one saved with a new name) line by line, asking yourself "Who cares?"

b. If a line, phrase, or section is irrelevant for the targeted position, modify or delete it. (This is why it's essential that you leave your master resume intact and work with the one saved under a new name.)

c. Avoid controversial topics (e.g., hunting) or affiliations (e.g., political or religious) that might unnecessarily and unintentionally have a negative impact on the hiring manager's first impression. However, if the transferable skills from those activities are relevant, consider referring to them in a more generic way (e.g., managed the Facebook presence for a successful political campaign).

5. Refer to the job ad and all of the research you have gathered about the targeted organization and the specific job. Potential sources include the organization's website, annual report, press releases, or online networking presence (e.g., LinkedIn).

a. Be sure your targeted resume includes the employer's own words. This is particularly important if there is a chance your resume will be processed electronically, based on a keyword search (e.g., MS Office 2007, bookkeeper, customer service).

b. Match the employer's tone and the organization's brand (e.g., use language and style that are appropriately conservative, creative, or energetic).

## Resume Styles

There are four distinct resume styles: chronological, functional, combination, or curriculum vitae (CV). Choose the one that works best for you each time you create a targeted resume.

A chronological resume organizes your information by date, with the most recent first. Preferred by most employers, this type of resume will work well if you have had relevant education and work experience with a clear progression of responsibility and accomplishments.

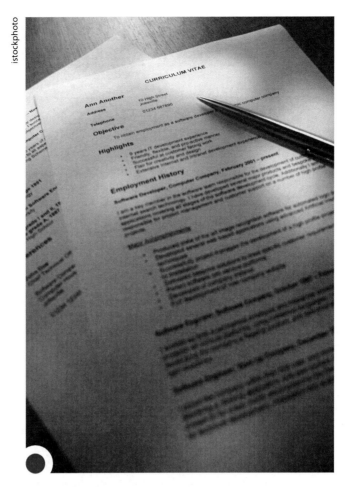

*There are a variety of resume styles; choose a style that works for you.*

A functional resume showcases your relevant skills that may not be clearly attached to relevant work or school experiences. Purely functional resumes tend to worry employers; they wonder what you are trying to hide by not providing dates and specific job titles or education.

A combination resume, just as its name implies, offers the best of both chronological and functional approaches. Generally, relevant skills and personal characteristics are highlighted on the first page of a combination resume, supported by chronological detail about work and school experiences on the second page. This format allows applicants to paint a clear picture of their qualifications (i.e., forming a positive first impression) before the employer has the chance to form a different image based on an apparently unrelated job title or degree. Combination resumes can be particularly effective for career changers and for students who have had a series of summer or part-time jobs that developed relevant transferable skills but, on the surface, don't seem closely related to the targeted job.

Although the term CV is often used interchangeably with resume, within academic and some professional communities, it has a distinctly different meaning. Generally, a CV is longer than a resume and provides reverse chronological lists of relevant professional experiences such as courses taught, conference presentations, publications, and professional service on boards and committees.

Tip *You only have 20–40 seconds on average to keep a resume reviewer's attention.*

## Resume Format

Your resume must be easy to skim, with the most compelling information near the top of the first page. Use clear headings and bullets to make sure relevant information is quickly accessible. In English, we read top to bottom, left to right. Therefore, the left margin is the second most significant "real estate" on your resume, after the top third of page 1. Don't clutter that important left margin with dates. Instead use it for job titles or previous employers. Decide on your structure based on what your targeted employer is likely to be most impressed by; once you select a structure, apply it consistently throughout.

Human resource (HR) professionals typically review a lot of resumes. Therefore, surveys about their preferences provide us with important information about how to effectively structure a resume. Over the years, we have drawn from many such surveys and focus groups. Table 10.1 presents highlights about what most of these HR professionals and hiring managers have indicated they prefer.

Resumes come in very different formats and styles. Ensure that you have a clear understanding of the format required for each job you are applying for. Some organizations specify a preferred format; they may want resumes to be submitted on paper, by email (as attachments or embedded within the body of a message), or online (either by attaching a document or by entering information into a standardized form). Using a standardized format makes it easier for the hiring committee to find the exact information they need to inform their decisions. Similar to completing a job application, it is essential to include everything requested and carefully follow the specified format.

| TABLE 10.1 | Resume Features Preferred by HR Professionals and Hiring Managers | |
|---|---|
| **Feature** | **Description** |
| Clear and concise | • Relevant information is easy to find<br>• Resume is one to two pages |
| Error-free | • No typing or spelling mistakes<br>• Use of consistent fonts, spacing, and margins |
| Targeted | • Doesn't seem like it was written for another job |
| Chronological | • Not purely functional (i.e., dates and details are important) |
| Compelling | • Attention-grabbing<br>• Makes a great first impression |
| Readable | • Generally, 12-point fonts that are commonly available on most computers (e.g., Times New Roman or Arial) are recommended (fonts should be no smaller than 10-point) |
| Action Verbs | • Begins each bullet with an action (e.g., conducted, developed, coordinated, improved, negotiated) |

Tip    *Expectations about resume styles and components change across countries. A North American resume is generally no more than two pages, doesn't include a photo, and excludes personal information such as date of birth and marital status. In many other countries, all those items would be expected on a resume.*

If submitting your resume on paper, use good quality paper in a neutral color (i.e., crisp white, ivory, or gray). Slightly off-white colors tend to stand out in a stack of plain paper documents. If you have access to a color printer, consider creating a letterhead-style header and using subtle color for headings and subheadings (e.g., dark blue headings with black text). Print your resume single-sided and do not staple the pages (for ease of photocopying by the employer). Your name should be clearly indicated on each page.

If submitting your resume by email, consider phoning ahead to find out how it will be processed. Some organizations block email attachments; it may be necessary to cut and paste your resume into the body of your message. There are compatibility issues between some PC and MAC computers and between older and newer computers. Excessive formatting, especially with the newest versions of a software package, may be unreadable by your recipient. To ensure readability, use a common font such as Times New Roman or Arial that most software packages will recognize, and avoid unnecessary graphics or unusual bullets. Keep in mind that many individuals will be previewing their emails on hand-held devices such as smart phones, iPods, or other personal digital assistants (PDAs). To ensure that your message does not get deleted, the subject line must be clear and the initial part of the message brief enough to convey the key points, convincing the recipient to save your resume for an in-depth look back at the office.

In some cases—for example, to cut and paste or upload information into an online form—it will be necessary to convert your resume into a plain text format by using a .txt extension in the document name. In many software programs, this can be accomplished by simply saving the file as a text document; in MS Word, choose File/Save as/Save as type/Plain text). Another option is to open the text editor provided with your computer (e.g., NotePad in Windows; SimpleText in Macintosh), then cut and paste your formatted resume into it.

Before sending an email to a potential employer, try sending it to a friend to see how the formatting looks to the recipient. There may be embedded characters that don't show up on your screen but that fill several lines at the beginning of the document on someone else's. When converting to plain text, it's generally a good idea to remove all bolding, to substitute asterisks for bullets, and to use one consistent font throughout.

For any resume or application that will be processed electronically, appropriate key words are essential. Consider placing a key word summary immediately after your contact information; use nouns and sector or occupation-specific acronyms, provide academic qualifications, and list relevant personal characteristics such as languages. Match your key words as closely as possible to the employer's own language; that is, incorporate specific words from an ad, job description, or information on the corporate website. One caution here is to be sure that you draw on the employer's language without plagiarizing information. You can avoid this by paraphrasing rather than using direct quotes from the employer's brochures and/or websites. Similar to conducting an Internet search using a search engine such as Google, appropriate key words will ensure that your resume surfaces as one that is a close match for the employer's criteria when retrieving resumes from the organization's recruitment database. Because a resume processed electronically loses the traditional advantages of a creative look and a persuasive tone, to be considered at all, your message will need to be captured in key words that match the search criteria used. Remember that search engines are literal—they will not "read between the lines" and make assumptions about the transferability of your experiences.

Once your resume is retrieved, it also needs to be appealing to the reader. At this point, all of the formatting techniques for paper-based resumes will have impact; ensure a consistent structure, attend to the order in which information is presented, use action verbs, and clearly document your accomplishments.

If you choose to post your resume on Internet-based job boards, such as Monster and Workopolis, be cautious about privacy and the potential for identity theft. Consider removing identifying information except for your name and creating a new email address specifically for job search purposes. The key, of course, is to remember to check this new address regularly or have messages automatically forwarded to your regular email account.

You may also find it useful to post your resume on your own career-related website. Rather than mixing your career and personal information, it is generally best to keep this separate. If you provide a link to your online resume, a potential employer is quite likely to look elsewhere on your site. This will form part of the first impression you create; therefore, managing your online presence is crucial.

## Cover Letters

There are diverse opinions about whether or not cover letters are necessary or important; some decision makers highly value them while others ignore them altogether. The key is to ensure that your cover letter adds value (i.e., it complements your resume) but that your resume can stand alone if necessary (i.e., there is no essential information available only in your cover letter).

Use the first paragraph of your cover letter to link yourself to the organization (why you are writing). In the second paragraph, describe your interest and fit, explaining how what you have to offer meets their needs and what has impressed you about the organization. The third paragraph provides an opportunity to indicate or acknowledge next steps; in the case of an unsolicited application, mention that you will follow up by phone next week or that you will be in town at the beginning of the month and hope to set up some meetings.

Keep the overall look of your cover letter consistent with your resume—this is part of developing your personal brand. If you created a header with your contact information for your resume, use the same header on your cover letter, forming the impression of personal letterhead.

Ensure that your cover letters are targeted; it is easy to recognize "form letters" and they rarely add value. Instead, use your letter as an opportunity to let your personality shine through and to showcase your research about the organization you are applying to. Inform the potential employer why you have chosen this particular job or organization: What impresses you about their website? Current projects? Reputation? Use strong, confident language; avoid words like "I hope" or "I feel." If you have relevant quotes from your references—and permission to use them—include some in your cover letter to provide third-party evidence of your claims (e.g., "A recent client wrote..." or "My marketing professor complimented me on...").

If possible, address your cover letter to a specific person; check the organization's website or phone the office if necessary. Make sure names are spelled accurately and preferred titles are used (e.g., Dr., Ms.). Many people have clear preferences and may become annoyed with an incorrect salutation; clearly, this wouldn't contribute to a great first impression! Don't make assumptions about gender; initials don't provide that information and many first names (e.g., Kim, Jasjit, Pat) are used by both men and women. If, despite all your best efforts, you can't find an individual's name, address the letter generically—for example, Dear Hiring Committee or Dear Operations Manager—or use a memo format and avoid the "Dear" line entirely.

## Effective Writing

Your resumes, cover letters, and any other written communication such as emails, thank you letters, and work samples all contribute to the impression that your potential employer is forming. Your writing should be professional, error-free, clear, and concise. Explain acronyms on first use; although they may be common within a specific occupation or sector, be aware that HR professionals, recruiters, and managers may have different professional backgrounds than you. Your written communication must be generic enough to be understood and interpreted by an outsider but specific enough to ensure that an insider is impressed by your relevant knowledge and competencies. Before sending any written documents, ask a friend or colleague to proofread for you.

Although it may be tempting to engage a professional to write your resumes and cover letters, these documents will generally work better for you if your own "voice" comes through. That doesn't mean that you can't get support from an expert in terms of structure, organization, and proofreading. However, first describe your accomplishments and personal characteristics from your own perspective, interspersing the employer's specific terms where they fit your experience. Only then, after you have anchored what you believe is important to say, consider asking for help in polishing the final drafts.

Use headings, paragraphs, bullets, or other organizational strategies to ensure your information is easy for a reader to understand. Remember that your resume, cover letter, application, and related emails are sales tools as well as informative documents; use adjectives and rich descriptions to make them persuasive. Provide hard data wherever possible (e.g., grew membership by 23% during first year as association president; negotiated 10% discount on office supplies).

## Career Portfolios

Career portfolios are becoming increasingly popular as a tangible way to document and communicate career accomplishments. Artists, actors, and architects have used portfolios for years; now they are becoming standard for other

*Create a positive impression with your written documents.*

istockphoto

occupations as well. Many high schools and post-secondary institutions require students to build a career portfolio as a graduation requirement.

Although much attention may be paid to the format of a portfolio—for example, web-based, binder, portable file box, or a more artistic representation using scrapbooking techniques—the reality is that most employers will not ask to see your portfolio and, if you present it, won't take the time to look through the whole collection. It makes more sense to use your portfolio as a personal organizing tool, set up in a way that it will be easy for you to find what you need for specific purposes (e.g., a specific sample of work for a job interview, a transcript to support an application to grad school, or contact information for a reference you want to use for a particular opportunity).

Similar to your master resume, if you are building a portfolio for your own personal use, there is no need to worry about an attractive format and no need to limit the number of items you include. Rather, begin to collect any information that may potentially be useful in your future job searches and select a framework or filing system that makes intuitive sense to you; the goal is to ensure that you can find exactly what you need without having to waste time looking for it.

To get you started, here is a list of potential portfolio items. Some may not be relevant for you; others, that may present wonderful evidence of your qualifications, may not be listed here:

- Academic documents (certificates, diplomas, transcripts)
- Agendas or programs, especially those listing you as event organizer or presenter
- Marketing materials (brochures from programs or projects you contributed to)
- Performance reviews or evaluations
- Photographs, if they illustrate an accomplishment supporting your application
- Plaques or group awards (include a photocopy or photo)
- Publications such as newsletter/newspaper stories about you or your projects, brochures
- Recognition from others (awards, references, thank you letters, or emails)
- Resume or professional profile/biography
- Work samples (excerpts of school projects, published articles, photos of projects)
  - Be sure you have permission to share work samples, especially if the project was proprietary or contained confidential information. Sometimes you can remove the private contents but still showcase the format of the report you wrote.

Depending on your comfort with computers, your preference may be to organize your portfolio as a computer-based file or as a website. The key is to be intentional about saving evidence of your accomplishments that can support future job applications and career conversations.

## Impression Management

Similar to how "branding" contributes to an organization's marketing strategy, defining and consistently using your own personal brand will contribute to your successful job search. Just as organizations re-brand to approach a new target market, so too might your personal brand need to be adjusted as you transition from school to work or between different occupations or sectors.

There are four distinct arenas within which to manage your professional image: on paper, by phone, in person, and online. Tips for impression management in each of these areas are presented in the following sections.

## Paper

As described in the resume and cover letter section of this chapter, potential employers will form an impression of you through your written communication. They will notice whether it is clear, concise, error-free, and interesting. Does your email address convey the image you hope to create? Consider choosing subtle colors, appropriate fonts, and attractive design elements to ensure that your documents stand out from the rest, while portraying a professional look.

## Phone

As previously discussed, consider carefully which phone numbers to provide to potential employers. Your voicemail should be clear and professional. Whenever you answer the phone (day, night, or weekend), assume that it could be a call from a potential employer. If using a phone that others may answer (e.g., a home phone or a number shared with roommates or family members), get their commitment to support your professional image by answering the phone appropriately and taking a detailed message if necessary.

## In Person

What is considered appropriate workplace language and attire changes quite dramatically across occupations, sectors, and even levels within an organization. As you develop your personal brand, choose a style that will fit within the specific organizations you are targeting but is also a good personal fit for you; although it's possible to "be someone else" in a job interview, it's very difficult to be painted into a corner where you can't be yourself long term. As you research occupations and organizations, notice how people dress, interact, and speak. You'll naturally be attracted to some organizations more than others. However, recognize that some of the people you encounter in the workplace have earned the right over time to their unique, perhaps somewhat eccentric, personas. Be constantly aware of the professional image you hope to project; if in doubt, for interviews and the first few days of work (i.e., as you build those important first impressions), err on the conservative side.

Remember, it is not just your clothing that contributes to your personal brand; consider how your hair, scents, shoes, piercings, tattoos, accessories, and general hygiene either support or detract from the impression you hope to create. Similarly, it is important for you to understand workplace etiquette; what is considered acceptable or rude changes subtly across organizations, regions, and cultures. Observe, ask questions, and find a well-respected "cultural informant" who is willing to be honest with you about what is working, what is not, and how to effectively manage the impression you are creating.

Finally, carefully consider the key messages that you want to convey when you meet someone in person—whether at a networking event, a job interview, or your first days at work. Adjust your elevator statement or 30-second commercial. You will have different key messages for different audiences; however, be strategic about

*Manage your online presence.*

the words you use that will contribute to the impression others form of you. Integrating key words, trends, and your knowledge of current workplace realities will convey the message that you fit and have high potential to contribute.

## Online

It's also important to consider your online presence. Have you "Googled" your name lately? Potential employers and recruiters likely have, as they were short-listing interview candidates. Consider the impression they may have formed as they looked at the associations you are linked to, reviewed your Facebook profile, or checked out your personal website or blog. There have been many high-profile examples of how an online presence has worked well (e.g., President Obama's successful campaign) or not (e.g., when another presidential hopeful's young daughter publicly endorsed Obama rather than her own Dad as a presidential candidate). There are countless resources to help you manage your online presence; just Google "online impression management" "job search" for a few to get you started.

## Managing References

Your references will also impact the impression you create; select them wisely! Do some "due diligence" before submitting a reference's contact information—the best reference for one position might be the kiss of death for another if that individual doesn't have a good reputation with the decision makers at your new organization.

## Impression Management: What's Working? What's Not?

ACTIVITY 10.2    Use the following spaces to record some of the reflections about the impression you hope to form. What's currently working and what's not in each of these arenas? (E.g., Phone: What's working? My voicemail has a professional greeting. What's not working? Sometimes my roommate does not take detailed messages.)

| Format | What's Working? | What's Not? |
|---|---|---|
| Paper | | |
| Phone | | |
| In Person | | |
| Online | | |

Don't make assumptions that someone will speak highly of you; if in doubt, ask directly, especially about areas of potential concern (e.g., "What will you say about why I left the organization?" or "How will you answer a question about my weaknesses?"). Some individuals are generally cautious or reserved; they'll never speak highly of anyone—but your potential employer won't know that. Choose references who will speak honestly, enthusiastically, and positively about your work.

Select references who have specific and relevant knowledge about you. Your favorite professor may not be able to speak in detail about your career accomplishments; the supervisor from your summer job in retail sales may not be able to speak about your competencies as a social worker; your best friend's dad, despite his impressive position within the industry, may know nothing about your ability to network computers. Such contacts may be wonderful for opening doors as you research opportunities; professional references, however, need to be able to speak in a concrete way about your ability to perform the specific job you've applied for.

Do not be afraid to coach your references. They may need reminders of your specific accomplishments while you worked for them or when you were a student in their classes; there's no reason to expect a past supervisor, instructor, or colleague to recall your past accomplishments in vivid detail without some prompting. If you have been building a career portfolio, it will be useful at this point to help you identify and document accomplishments related to each of your selected references.

Also, inform your references of professional development and career accomplishments since you left their employ (or since you finished the course you took from them). It can be helpful to give your references a clearly organized table listing key job requirements in one column and specific details about how you match those requirements in the other (see Table 10.2). Also, provide your references with the targeted resume submitted for the job you are asking them to endorse you for.

Be sure to check in with your references each time you plan to use their names. Confirm that their contact information is current, that they'll be available to respond quickly to requests, and that they are clear about the specific job you are applying for. They might choose different stories or examples, for instance, if they know you are applying for an accounting job with a national grocery retailer versus a hotel chain.

| TABLE 10.2 Linking Accomplishments to Job Requirements ||
|---|---|
| **Job Requirements** | **My Qualifications/Accomplishments** |
| | |
| | |
| | |
| | |
| | |
| | |
| | |
| | |

You may occasionally need a reference on very short notice; if your best reference is out of town, it may be helpful to have some written recommendations on hand to share with your potential employer. Also, a good letter of recommendation written soon after a major accomplishment will likely provide richer detail than if a reference is asked to speak about the accomplishment several years later.

Finally, if your references are from a different time zone or may answer the phone in a different language, make it easy for your potential employer to connect. Provide exact dialing instructions (complete with country code and, ideally, with a direct line or specific extension). Calculate time zones (e.g., "If you phone at 4 p.m. here, you will be likely to reach him in the office because it will be 8 a.m. there"). And, if necessary, provide key local language phrases written out phonetically that will get the right person on the phone in a foreign country.

## Summary

This chapter has focused on the logistics of turning your career possibilities into realities through creating effective resumes and cover letters, building a career portfolio to document your accomplishments, branding and impression management, and selecting and coaching your references.

Revisiting Jon Hiroto's unique situation in our case example introduced at the beginning of the chapter, it's easy to see that all of these tasks will be important considerations for him. As you'll recall, Jon doesn't have any paid work experience; however, he does have lots of transferable skills from his leadership positions and international lifestyle. Ideally, he has held on to relevant certificates and school projects, providing evidence of his accomplishments. Realistically, however, he may have saved very little; people who relocate internationally generally purge before each move, and what they do have is likely to be buried in a box in storage. Therefore, as part of his job search preparation, Jon may need to strategically gather some work samples and reference letters; he may also find it helpful to take on specific projects that will result in great references and evidence of his skills. Jon's references may be scattered across the globe; he may need to reconnect with them, update them on his career goals, and provide them with a current resume. As Jon's career interests are international and his network is already global, he may benefit from constructing a professional online presence with a blog, a LinkedIn profile, and a web-based career portfolio and resume. Depending on the country he chooses to work in, Jon will need to clarify resume or CV expectations. Jon, like all students transitioning from school to work, will need to build his professional "brand" and customized job search tools to support it. If he begins six months to a year before graduation, he will have plenty of time to prepare for a successful post-graduation career.

## Questions for Reflection and Discussion

1. In what ways are your challenges similar to Jon's? In what ways are they different?

2. From a career flow perspective, how will ensuring that you have the right tools in place impact your experience of flow as you begin looking for work or prepare to reposition your career?

3. Which of the tools and strategies described in this chapter—resume, cover letter, career portfolio, impression management, references, and so on—will be easiest for you to prepare? Which will be the most challenging? What's the first step you will take to get them in place?

## Additional Resources

Doyle, A. (n.d.). *Dressing for success: How to dress for an interview.* Retrieved July 29, 2009, from http://jobsearch.about.com/od/interviewsnetworking/a/dressforsuccess.htm. Provides tips on interview attire to contribute to effective first impressions, with specific examples of appropriate men's and women's attire.

Doyle, A. (n.d.). *Requesting letters of recommendation: Requesting references.* Retrieved July 29, 2009, from http://jobsearch.about.com/od/referencesrecommendations/a/recommendation.htm. In this informative article, Doyle addresses who to ask for a reference and how to ask. Links to other resources are also provided, including sample reference letters.

Kimeldorf, M. (1999). *Portfolio library.* Retrieved July 29, 2009, from www.amby.com/kimeldorf/p_mk-toc.html. Martin Kimeldorf is well known for his work with career portfolios. This site provides numerous resources on portfolios including tips and samples.

Morris Associates Inc. (n.d.). *Resume turnons and turnoffs: What readers do and don't like.* Retrieved July 29, 2009, from http://www.rcjobs.com/issues/1_1/seeker_resources/17-1.html. This article presents survey results from 213 government and corporate HR managers and recruiters from the greater Washington, D.C. area on what they prefer and dislike in resumes.

Weiss, T. (2008). *Entering the workforce: Give your career a flying start.* Retrieved July 29, 2009, from www.forbes.com/2008/03/26/workplace-dress-behavior-lead-careers-cx_tw_0327etiquette.html. Provides practical tips and insights for those important first few weeks at a new job.

" Success depends upon previous preparation, and without such preparation there is sure to be failure. "

—*Confucius*

# Engaging the Search: Generating Leads, Networking, Interviewing, and Making a Successful Transition

## OBJECTIVES

This chapter focuses on the job search and related skills. After reading this chapter, you will be able to:

- Generate work opportunities
- Network effectively
- Master the interview process
- Successfully transition to the next stage of your career

## CASE STUDY

As Jasjit Singh registered for her final semester at college, she was both excited and terrified. She'd returned to school 4 years ago, soon after her 17-year marriage ended; as part of her divorce agreement, Jasjit's ex-husband fully paid for her college education. Since their first child was born the year they were married, Jasjit had remained home caring for their children and her husband's mother. After his mother died 5 years ago, Jasjit's husband decided he wanted a divorce; their four children were all in high school at the time.

Between child support and alimony, Jasjit has been able to continue to live in the family home. However, now two of their four children are away at college, and the other two will graduate this year and next. After that, her alimony will end, child

Thomas Northcut/Riser/Getty Images

support will transfer directly to the children as long as they are in school, and Jasjit will need to fully support herself. Even with a good job in her field, Jasjit will not be able to afford to maintain her family home on her own and she realizes that it will be far too big for her to live in alone. Some days she gets excited about the thought of buying a new home that suits her own tastes; other days, she is angry that a life that she once loved has been so disrupted. Jasjit doesn't know whether she should stay in the same community so that when her children come to visit, it feels like "home" to them or if she should take this opportunity to make a fresh start somewhere else. She has a little over a year to decide; waiting for her final child to finish high school, however, is impacting her choices for her own career. She doesn't know whether to look for part-time or contract work for the year just to get some experience, or to look seriously for a "real" job that could result in a longer-term commitment to her current location. As Jasjit doesn't even know where she'll be living a year and a half from now, the uncertainty is almost overwhelming at times.

*Jasjit's story highlights the complexity of school-to-work transitions. This chapter provides strategies for generating specific work opportunities, mastering the interview process, and navigating challenging transitions to result in a fully satisfying next step on your career journey.*

## Generating Work Opportunities

This is the culmination of your career planning and work search preparation, building on your self-reflections, goal setting, and comprehensive research. After you've developed basic tools such as resumes, cover letters, and career portfolios, you are ready to respond to specific work opportunities.

This step will be most effective if you have a clear goal in mind—work that is realistic, interesting, and worth actively pursuing. Perhaps counterintuitively, being open to "any job at all" is unlikely to generate specific leads. It's like being open to going to any university: where would you apply? Or moving into any apartment: where would you start looking?

So, before moving forward, revisit your goals and action plans. If your goal is a bit fuzzy, review or revise self-assessment activities you've completed. It may be time to face your fears or re-establish supports. In essence, sometimes it is necessary to spend time in the stillwaters of career flow: charting your course to brace yourself for the whitewater that tends to accompany transitional times.

Once you have a clear goal in mind, it is time to generate concrete leads. Begin by revisiting your career research and capturing everything relevant to your chosen direction. Visit websites for the organizations that interest you; some may have specific career opportunity sections. Also, Google the occupation, industry, or organization name for recent press releases or news items; although these generally won't list job openings, they can provide important information about emerging trends, funding or policy changes, stock prices, new projects, or changes in leadership. For larger organizations that tend to be in the news daily, narrow your search (e.g., "organization name" "press release" "month year").

Also, subscribe to listservs that share job openings, for example, through professional associations you joined as a student. Do a current Google search using the occupation, industry, or organization names you have selected and limit the search with your preferred region.

Craig's List has quickly become an important place to find job listings; although not specifically set up as a job board, many employers find it far more effective for recruitment than other traditional services. Go to www.craigslist.org, select a preferred region, narrow it further to the nearest city, select "Jobs," and then click on the category that most closely matches the specific kind of work you are interested in.

Create a list of relevant career fairs in your area and plan to attend some; Google "career fair" in your region and "month year." Aside from being a source of current openings, career fairs can provide general information about occupations, sectors, or organizations that interest you and an opportunity to talk to an employee to get an insider's look. Keep in mind that the insights are from a corporate representative's or recruiter's perspective; as his or her role at the career fair is to "sell" careers, you are not getting an unbiased view.

Depending on your specific career goals and the current economy, you might also find it helpful to register with one or more recruiting firms; avoid signing a contract with a recruiter that prevents you from working with other recruiters or accepting a job that you find on your own. Recruiters may have exclusive access to some local employers (i.e., all hiring is done through the recruiter); because they are constantly engaged in hiring, they will also have a good sense of the current trends in your field. Feedback from recruiters about your resume, experience, and overall presentation in terms of industry or organizational fit may be invaluable; be aware, however, that most recruiters have standard resume formats and their requests for changes may be specifically for their own internal use.

Temporary job placement firms may also be an effective way to connect to the workforce. Short-term contracts provide you with an insider's view of an organization (or, perhaps, several organizations). Some employers have a policy of hiring full-time employees only from their temporary workers. Placement firms generally have clear policies about how employers can buy you out of their contract if they want to bring you on board before the original term has ended.

## *Contacts and Leads*

**ACTIVITY 11.1**

Use the table below to record specific sources of job leads within your field. For example, once you identify an organization that interests you, write the organization's website address in the corresponding space.

| Type of Resource | Specific Sources |
|---|---|
| Organization's Website | |
| News and Press Release | |
| Listservs | |
| Job Boards | |
| Career Fairs | |
| Recruiters | |
| Placement Firms | |
| Other | |

# Networking Effectively

Your network will be a useful support at all stages of the career flow process. In the planning stage, your networking efforts were focused on gathering background information to inform your career decisions. During the implementing stage, however, your networking will be more targeted as you seek out contacts in specific occupations, industries, organizations, professional associations, or geographic regions to access any specific job leads they may know about. Although statistics vary according to industry, region, and economic conditions, it is generally accepted that about 80 percent of job openings are filled through networking; that is, the openings may not have been advertised and, even if they were, the individual hired was referred by a contact. It is essential to tap into this "hidden" job market if you want to maximize your chances of finding great work.

To begin this new stage of networking, revisit the map of your existing personal and professional network. You may have created one when reflecting on your sources of support (in the self-clarity stage) or conducting career research (in the planning stage). If not, use your contact lists—within your email system, mobile phone, Facebook, Twitter, or MSN account—to begin your data mining.

Tip     *Your network will be most effective if it is nurtured and not just activated at crucial times.*

Activate your network by reconnecting with key contacts, updating them on your progress and career decisions, and asking for their insights about who to talk to and where to find current work opportunities. If you are in regular contact with your contacts, they won't be surprised to know you're looking for work. In fact, they may already have mentioned you to key contacts who they know might be hiring. Be sure to keep your network up-to-date regarding your changing interests and goals, major accomplishments, and job search process.

*"Luck is what happens when preparation meets opportunity."* —Seneca

Psychologist John Krumboltz (2004), in his work on happenstance, said that uncertainty is natural and plans emerge and evolve. The key, however, is to remain curious and active; you are far more likely to generate work opportunities at a networking event (or even a sports activity or family dinner) than if you are chained to your computer passively waiting for an employer to notice the resume you posted online. Many individuals can identify "lucky breaks" in their careers; however, as Roman philosopher Seneca has been credited for saying, "Luck is what happens when preparation meets opportunity."

To increase the likelihood of lucky breaks, formulate specific requests for your network contacts (e.g., "Do you know anyone working at XYZ company, ideally in marketing?"). Your preliminary conversations will likely take place with people whom you connect with casually on a daily basis; although they're unlikely to be in a position to hire you—and may not even have direct contact with your potential employer—their referrals will be *warm* rather than *cold* calls.

At this next level of networking, you are much more likely to be moving closer to people who *will* have direct leads, so be sure to ask for those leads. The good news is that, again, your next calls will be warm rather than cold. Although with those closest to you, it's unlikely that you would use an elevator statement (i.e., a short description of what you want and how you're qualified), you may find it helpful to write out some key points to cover with your second and third level contacts as these will be people who you don't know personally, or at least not very well.

Do not wait for a job to be advertised. Make a list of all employers of interest to you and contact them directly to see if they are considering hiring. Ask potential employers if they are available for an informational interview. Even if employers that interest you don't have a suitable job opening, some may have other contacts in their professional networks looking for someone with your skills. Keep in mind the high number of unadvertised jobs and the various formats they may take: parental leaves, relocation, expansion, seasonal hiring, new projects. Many employers have even created new positions after meeting an interesting individual and seeing great potential.

During this active stage of work search, attend as many networking events as you can fit into your weeks (and, of course, can afford). To effectively network at events, act like a host rather than a guest. Proactively introduce yourself; if you know others at the event, introduce them to each other. Use small talk to find commonalities but focus on engaging in authentic, rich interactions. Be positive and respectful; spend more time listening than talking. Create a professional impression by demonstrating cultural competency, industry knowledge, and a sincere interest in the sector-related conversations. If alcohol is served, either avoid it altogether or make one drink last through the whole event. Your goal is to generate leads, sound professional and articulate, and remember subtle details that come up in a myriad of conversations; you need to remain sharp and focused. Aim to leave each conversation with a concrete lead, referral, tip, or new perspective. Sometimes your contacts will think of important information after you leave; be sure to give them your resume or business card with your specific information request on the back, or offer to follow up by email if that would be more convenient for them.

Nurture your network; networking that is one-sided, that is, it's all about you, gets stale very quickly. Effective networking is not a contest won by collecting the most business cards or having the most populated database. Rather, it is based on mutually rewarding relationships as you exchange information, insights, leads, and support. Be sure to follow through on leads from your network and update those who have given you leads on your progress. Effective networking will continue to benefit you throughout your career by opening doors, sharing industry updates, providing candid feedback, and, through relevant connections, enhancing your professional image.

Expand your horizons. Engage your network in helping you to consider all possibilities. You may be focused on securing full-time work; would two part-time contracts or a short-term project potentially work? Being open to alternatives could unleash countless possibilities; employers who don't have a full-time position in the budget might consider bringing you on board on a part-time or contractual basis.

Are you committed to a specific geographical location? If not, begin your search within a circle close to home and gradually widen it. Take a similar approach with other cities or countries where you have contacts in place (e.g., if you are based in Nebraska but have family in Tennessee, it may make more sense to expand your work search to Tennessee than to Kansas, even though Kansas is geographically closer).

As you learn details about specific work opportunities, revisit your self-assessments to check for a good fit. Does the specific opportunity capitalize on your strengths and skills? Does it interest and intrigue you? Will your key reasons for working, that is, your work values, be satisfied? Does the organizational culture suit your personal style? How will accepting this job impact the significant people in your life? Does it provide opportunities for ongoing career development? Does it fit with your leisure activities and lifestyle priorities?

# Mastering the Interview Process

Your active pursuit of relevant leads has paid off and you have been invited for an interview! To prepare, it will be helpful to know a bit about the structure of the interview process. The following sections provide information about some types of interviews that you might encounter; it's not unusual that the hiring process will involve more than one interview, so you may experience several different interview styles while pursuing the same job lead. It's also important to recognize the distinct stages in the hiring process; later in this section, you'll find tips on how to create a great impression before the interview begins, during the interview, and after it ends.

## Types of Interviews

Interview styles and formats vary greatly, depending on the purpose, stage of the interview process, sector or industry, and each interviewer's skills and preferences. There are many good books and websites to help with interview preparation. This section will be limited to a brief overview of the most common types of interviews: screening and assessment, panel, telephone or video, situational or targeted-behavioral, and group.

Knowing the type of interview to expect and, ideally, a bit about the interviewers will help you prepare for your interview and showcase your relevant talents. Take time to research this crucial background information by connecting with others who have recently been hired or interviewed by the organizations you have been invited to interview with. If you don't have relevant contacts, take a few minutes to gather relevant details from the individual who scheduled your interview. Ask whether you will be interviewed individually or with a group, by a panel or a single interviewer. Clarify the interview process: Is this a screening interview? Will there be any assessments? If successful in this interview, what are the next steps? If there will be a series of interviews, how many interviews are typical? Who is involved in the interview process: Coworkers? The hiring manager? A recruiter?

A member of the HR team? Don't be afraid to ask questions; there is such variance in interview formats that you can't possibly know what to expect without asking someone.

Your first interview with an employer is likely to be for screening and assessment purposes, to confirm that the claims on your resume are accurate. You may not even realize that you are being interviewed; screening may happen right at the booth at a career fair in what seems to be a completely casual and unfocused conversation with the recruiter. Similarly, later in the process, you may be invited to lunch or a social event; although such meetings may not seem like a real interview, it's important to recognize that all interactions with potential job candidates influence the decision-making process.

Expect a screening interview to include questions about your resume, past experience, and education. There may be questions to assess your knowledge or skills (i.e., an informal or semi-structured assessment process). There may also be formal or standardized assessments to complete; these could be to assess job-specific skills such as word-processing speed and accuracy and business math; soft skills such as critical thinking, honesty, and time orientation; or personal style preferences to assess fit for a specific role or team. Some interview assessments involve work simulations; for example, an "in basket" exercise is quite typical for assessing how managers juggle priorities. Other assessments are administered by external organizations; for example, a specific driver's license or safety certificate might be required before applicants will be "promoted" to the next interview stage.

In a global economy supported by technology, it is increasingly likely that one or more steps in the interview process will be conducted by email, telephone, or online. You may be asked to complete some online assessments prior to an interview, or you may need to dial-in to a teleconference or web-based meeting room (e.g., GoToMeeting) or log on to a voice over Internet protocol (VOIP) provider such as Skype). Just as you would be sure to allow extra time to get to an in-person interview, allow time to test out the technology and ensure it is working smoothly for you. If you are having any challenges, do not hesitate to ask for help. The person that set up the interview is likely quite comfortable guiding applicants through the process.

*Customize your interview answers to create a positive impression.*

Shutterstock

Of course, it is almost certain that you will also be interviewed in person, either by an individual or a panel of interviewers. There are significant differences between these two types of interviews. In an individual interview, you need to develop rapport with, and ultimately impress and persuade, one person. In a panel, on the other hand, rapport-building and making a positive impression is more challenging; it's quite possible that the interviewers come from diverse professional backgrounds, have very different personal styles, and may even have conflicting ideas about the personal characteristics of an ideal candidate. In either case, it's important that your responses are customized to the interviewers' knowledge of the sector and your occupation in particular. Recruiters and human resource professionals may be highly skilled in interviewing for interpersonal and transferable skills but may not have in-depth industry or job-specific knowledge. The hiring manager or a potential coworker, on the other hand, may have very specific questions about your technical expertise and ability to fit within the established team.

Cultural differences can also impact your interview success. In each interview, be aware of differing culture-based expectations about level of formality (e.g., use of first or last names), deference to age, eye contact, personal space, small talk, and the importance of group versus individual accomplishments. If you know in advance the cultural affiliations of your interviewers, cultural informants (i.e., people in your network who are from, or have significant experience with, different cultural backgrounds) may be helpful in alerting you to potential considerations. However, more likely, you'll have to make adjustments as you become aware of the interviewers' cultural expectations such as shaking hands when a hand is extended, standing until you are asked to sit down, or responding to small talk initiated by others.

Some interviews will require you to respond to hypothetical situations (e.g., "What would you do if…?"). More commonly, interviewers will be interested in what you *actually did* under similar circumstances (e.g., "Think about a time that _____ happened. What did you do when…?"). These are known as "targeted-behavioral" interviews, and they are based on an underlying belief that the best predictor of future behavior is past behavior. Although it's generally much easier to engage in hypothetical discussions about ideal situations, these tend to provide "book answers" and may not represent your real world attitudes and behaviors. Targeted-behavioral interviews, on the other hand, provide opportunities for you to share real examples of how you handled a challenge, crisis, conflict, or even an everyday workplace occurrence.

To prepare for targeted-behavioral questions, review your work, school, and general life experiences and identify two or three great "stories" that you want to incorporate into your interview. You may find it helpful to write out highlights of each story using the STAR (Situation, Task, Action, Result) model. Although you likely won't refer to your written story during the interview, the act of writing it out will help to refresh your memory with the details and make the example easier to recall during the interview. As the point of a STAR story is to provide evidence of how you work, ensure that the majority of the time spent telling your story is on your *action* (the A in STAR). Briefly describe the situation (allocate less than 10 percent of the story time); similarly, minimize your description of the task. However, spend about 75 percent of your time describing your role in the scenario, including how you made the decision about what to do, and why. Finally, briefly summarize your story with a memorable ending, highlighting the result and how it was directly linked to your actions. Some stories don't have perfect endings; in those cases, wrap up the story with what you learned from the experience and how it has impacted your approach to work ever since.

## STAR Stories Revisited

ACTIVITY 11.2

As you prepare for your job interview, use the space provided below to anchor two or three STAR stories. For example, Jasjit chose to share a story about a final paper she wrote on the topic of cultural diversity (situation). To research the paper, she had to interview three people from different cultures (task). She used her network of family, friends, and acquaintances to identify her interviewees, created a good rapport with the interviewees, completed all three interviews early, and left enough time to comfortably write and edit her paper (action/attitude). She earned 98 percent on that paper, and it resulted in her qualifying for a scholarship prize (result).

| Element / Interview Time | STAR Story #1 | STAR Story #2 |
|---|---|---|
| Situation 10% | | |
| Task 10% | | |
| Action / Attitude 75% | | |
| Result 5% | | |

Many organizations use a series of interviews to inform their employee selection process. Perhaps beginning with a screening interview, then an assessment interview, followed by a panel interview, this process allows potential employers to see job applicants under diverse circumstances, often on several different days. Generally each stage in the process further shortlists the candidate pool; it is usually the interviews near the end of the series that involve more senior members of the organization.

One increasingly popular type of interview involves bringing a group of candidates in at the same time. This can be disconcerting if you're not expecting it. However, it generally serves one of two purposes: (1) an efficient way to provide much of the standard interview information typically covered in the first interview or (2) an opportunity to see how you interact with a group of peers. If the purpose is efficiency, there is little you need to do except show up on time and look appropriate for the job. In this type of interview, the group format is simply to save interviewers' time so they are not repeating the same 10 minutes of information about the organization or the hiring process with each new candidate. However, if you realize the purpose is to facilitate interaction—for example, after you arrive at the interview, you are divided into groups and given a task to work on together—the best approach is to pretend you are already working for the organization and this is your project team. It is important to showcase your skills and knowledge, but not by discrediting or shaming another member of the team. Work cooperatively, share creative ideas, and take on the leadership role as appropriate.

## Stages in the Interview Process

When most people hear the word *interview* they think of the specific time they will be meeting directly with the interviewers. However, the interview *process* actually extends over a much longer period than that. This section provides tips and strategies for preparing for the interview (the pre-interview stage), managing successfully during the interview itself, and effectively using time after the interview for reflection and follow-up.

The *pre-interview stage* begins even before you apply for a job. Your networking, research, and job search activities generated a lead that seemed worth pursuing. The hiring manager or selection committee agreed; you seem like a good potential fit and you have been invited for an interview. This is important to keep in mind; any time you have been called for an interview, someone has already determined that you are suitable for the position (i.e., they already like you!).

As mentioned earlier, documenting some of your initial research can save you considerable time as you prepare for an interview. Keep good job search files; bookmark the websites of the organizations you have applied to, and keep track of your contacts (i.e., who do you know who knows something about this organization?). Before your interview, revisit the website and review your notes about the organization and the specific opening. Connect with your contacts; let them know you have been called for an interview, ask them questions you have about the organization or interview process, and request permission to use their names as references.

Using the STAR story framework, identify three or four relevant stories you'd like to introduce during the interview. Reflect on questions that have been problematic for you in the past or questions you simply hope they don't ask in the interview. Although there are countless lists of "problem questions" in books and on the Internet, the only real problem questions will be those that you don't have an acceptable answer for. The question itself isn't the problem; the problem is that your answer may reveal something you would rather the interviewers did not know.

 Tip  *Sometimes you will be given a choice of interview times; if possible, ask for the last one.*

Statistically, those interviewed last get the job far more often than others; of course, this number is skewed as, in many cases, the interview process ends once a suitable candidate has been found. Those interviewed first also have a better than average chance of getting the job. Interviews on Mondays and Fridays tend to result in less success; mornings are usually better than afternoons. However, if you are invited to attend an interview at a scheduled time, try to accommodate; far more important than the time or day of the week is how well you prepare for and perform during the interview. If you do have a legitimate reason why you can't attend during a requested time, be honest and express your sincere interest in being interviewed—and request an alternate appointment.

What happens as you arrive for your interview is also part of the interview process; the first impression you create is significant. There are things within your control to ensure that you make a positive first impression. Are you on time? Unflustered? Suitably dressed? Well rested? Calm and cheerful? Enthusiastic? Optimistic? Be aware that your first impression may begin long before you enter the interview room. Consider the quality of your resume and cover letter; the telephone call when you were invited to the interview; the individuals you encountered in the parking lot, elevator, or coffee shop in the lobby; and your introduction of yourself to the receptionist. All of these provide opportunities for your professionalism and personal style to shine through; they may significantly impact your interview success.

During the interview, there are several distinct phases: the opening, the body of the interview, and the closing. Understanding the expectations for each of these phases can impact your interview success.

In most cases, a warm smile and a firm handshake will get you off to a good start. Eye contact (with each interviewer if there is more than one) and a simple question about how the day has been going so far may help to establish rapport. Finding common ground will put you all at ease; consider introducing a piece of relevant information that you got from your research; for example, "I notice that you had a team in the run on Sunday; I was there with a group from our school."

Most interviews begin with "small talk," which is intended to make you, the candidate, feel comfortable. However, it can sometimes feel like the most awkward part of an interview, especially if the interviewers are not good at small talk or the candidates are not prepared for it and are looking for a hidden agenda in every question asked. Practice making small talk with friends and family members until it is comfortable and natural to keep a conversation going; avoid controversial topics such as politics or religion and specialized topics that not everyone may be able to speak comfortably about (e.g., sports, emerging technology). Keep in mind that interviewers know you may be nervous; what may surprise you is that they are likely nervous, too. Making a hiring decision is a big responsibility!

If you are well prepared, the body of the interview will likely flow smoothly. Generally the interview will focus on your knowledge, skills, and attitudes (KSAs) as they relate to the position. Consider bringing some tangible evidence of your accomplishments; if you have assembled a career portfolio, it may contain a relevant sample of your work, feedback from a client, or an article that showcases your contributions to a project. Although most employers won't be interested in reviewing your whole portfolio, bringing a few relevant components to use as examples can make your responses more memorable for interviewers.

It is important to understand that some interviews will be very structured so that scores can be compared across interview candidates, interviewers, and even remote locations. This may make the flow of the interview a bit awkward; an interviewer may ask a question that it seems like you already answered. Similar to an exam in school where you may have covered material in question 1 that would also be useful for question 3, it's important that you answer each question thoroughly in order to get full points. It is fine to address this, to make the redundancy more comfortable (e.g., "As I mentioned a few minutes ago, my experience in..."); however, be careful not to sound frustrated at having to repeat yourself. Rather, be sure your response adds value to the overall interview, and use the opportunity to share another example or to showcase a different skill.

Although there are many questions that interviewers are not legally allowed to ask in an interview—relating to age, marital status, family plans, first language, ethnic background, nationality, and so on—some interviewers haven't been trained in interview protocol and others may ask something they are curious about without even realizing the question is illegal. It is important, from your perspective, to know that it is *not* illegal to answer an illegal question. So, if you are comfortable answering the question, the best approach may be to simply answer it graciously rather than embarrass the interviewer about his or her interviewing skills. However, if you are uncomfortable answering the question or feel that it may be used to unjustly discriminate against you, consider answering the underlying question. For example, if asking about family status or plans, the interviewer is likely concerned about your availability. Consider responding with, "I realize that with a young team, daycare issues can result in time off work. However, I am from a large, supportive family—back-up daycare has never been an issue for any of my siblings and, I know if I ever needed it, supports would be in place for me."

There will be many nonverbal clues in your interview that indicate whether your responses are on track or not; use them to guide subsequent answers. For example, interviewers may be looking for key words; in a panel interview, you may notice all the panelists taking notes at the same moment. This likely indicates that your answer contained what they hoped for. On the other hand, you may notice your interviewer looking puzzled, frustrated, or disengaged. Rather than assuming you have no chance of getting the job, use such cues to get back on track. Explore the concern with a statement like, "It seems like my last answer may have been unclear. Can you tell me a bit about that so that I can help to clarify what I meant?"

Especially in panel interviews, be careful not to ignore an individual or subgroup. Although this is likely to be unintentional, review of thousands of mock interview tapes revealed that women as interviewers were acknowledged far less frequently than men. While interviewees typically responded graciously when the female interviewers asked specific questions, the women were almost completely ignored the rest of the time. Something to watch for!

The end of the interview is one of the most important parts because final impressions are long-lasting. Generally, an interview concludes with the interviewer asking, "Do you have any questions?" At this point, control of the interview has been handed to you, so make wise use of the opportunity. If some of the questions you prepared before the interview haven't been answered, ask them now; your questions might relate to the future direction of the organization or specific department (e.g., What changes are you expecting within the department over the next year?) or something that's particularly important to you (e.g., What kinds of professional development opportunities does the organization offer?). However, if all of your questions have already been answered, use this time to introduce relevant information that wasn't covered during the interview and to reconfirm your interest in the job. Leave an articulate and enthusiastic final impression.

Although the actual interview has ended, the interview *process* will continue until a final decision has been made and an offer extended to (and accepted by) the successful candidate. Be sure to follow up the interview with a thank you note or email; it's not uncommon that the person who follows up is the one who gets offered the job. Sometimes you will reflect on a better answer to one of the interview questions; you could expand on that response in a follow-up note. You may also have referred to an article or website during the interview; your follow-up could include a copy of the article or a web link. If significant time goes by between an interview and a decision, you might also follow up with relevant updates such as certificates or courses now complete, changes in availability, or new contact information. Following up in a way that is meaningful (and not simply pestering the potential employer) helps to keep your name and application at the top of the list.

However, do not stop your job search just because you have had a good interview; actively continuing your search may generate even better opportunities. Having several offers to choose from can make you a more attractive candidate to a potential employer and may tip the scales in terms of prompting an offer or negotiating a good compensation package. It is not necessary to accept a job offer the moment it is made; ask when the employer needs your decision and use that time to consult with family and mentors, compare the position to your self-assessment results, and reconnect with other potential employers to see if they are close to making a decision.

Optimism has been linked to both career success and job satisfaction (Neault, 2002). However, when it comes to generating leads and reflecting on job interviews, it's important to temper optimism with pragmatism. Although it may be tempting to hold out for the perfect job, sometimes accepting a less-than-perfect opportunity positions you well for next steps. With additional experience and an expanded network, you might be considered for internal openings or may be successful the next time you apply for a job that is just slightly out of reach right now.

With interview success comes a career transition, sometimes within an organization and sometimes to a new organization, and perhaps a new region. The next section will help you navigate career transitions as you encounter them.

## Supporting Transitions to Next Career Stages

There are many transitional periods in life where career planning takes on increased importance; some of these include school-to-work transitions, life role transitions, health challenges that necessitate a change in work responsibilities, and relocation. Although some transitions such as graduation are long anticipated, others, such as a layoff, are unexpected and involuntary. Transitions can be challenging, exhilarating, unsettling, or refreshing; they can positively or negatively impact the sense of hope that is at the center of the career flow model. In the language of career flow, they may include whitewater, stillwater, jagged rocks, and perhaps even waterfalls! Several career management specialists have developed models to help put career transitions in perspective. Two of those models are presented here.

### Bridges Transition Model

William Bridges (2004) describes change as an external *event* and transition as an internal *process*. His transition model identifies three distinct stages—the ending, a neutral zone, and the new beginning—but he also addresses the pretransition stage as it can be an important time of anticipation and preparation.

Bridges suggests that tasks must be completed in each of the stages before the transition process can be successfully completed (see Figure 11.1). Tasks in the ending stage relate primarily to closure, for example, studying for and writing final exams, submitting term papers, applying for graduation, and giving notice to a landlord that you will be moving out. In the neutral zone, there may be a frenzy of chaotic activity as you explore possibilities and make new plans—a whitewater experience. However,

FIGURE 11.1    **Bridges Transition Model**

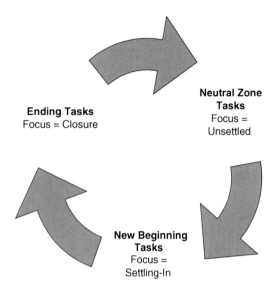

there may also be quiet times of reflection, self-assessment, recovery, and waiting—a stillwater experience. The neutral zone has been described as a bit like walking on quicksand: not very stable or secure. The new beginning is marked by feeling settled, regaining a sense of confidence and competence as you re-establish your life and career.

## *Transitioning through the Three Zones*

ACTIVITY 11.3    Use the table below to list tasks, anticipated challenges, and potential supports for each of the stages in the Bridges transition model: ending, neutral zone, and new beginning. For example, in the ending stage, Jasjit will need to sell her house; she anticipates that it may be challenging to negotiate a fair price but expects that her realtor will be a good support. Jasjit will transition to the neutral zone once her house is sold; her challenge will be finding a suitable new home. However, she has a friend who has offered to go looking with her. Her new beginning will involve settling into a new home (and perhaps a new community). She anticipates some loneliness after she moves but plans to start working and will also join a local fitness center to meet people in the community.

| Stage | Specific Tasks | Anticipated Challenges | Potential Supports |
|---|---|---|---|
| Ending | | | |
| Neutral | | | |
| Beginning | | | |

Shutterstock

*Emotions during a job search can feel just like riding a roller coaster.*

## Roller Coaster Model

Norm Amundson and Bill Borgen (1987) used a roller coaster metaphor to highlight the emotional reactions associated with job loss and unemployment; these reactions are quite similar to stages of grief or mourning, such as one experiences with other kinds of loss (e.g., loss of a loved one or loss of one's health). In the case example, Jasjit's story exemplifies this roller coaster as she reports feeling both excited and terrified. Searching for work can be a bit like paddling in whitewater, with emotions rapidly shifting from exhilaration (being selected for an interview) to despair (not being short-listed for a second one) to optimism (as a new opportunity surfaces that seems just right).

Both of these transition models acknowledge that transition is a process. A wide range of concerns and emotional reactions is normal during transitions. Being prepared for them by strengthening your supports and coping resources will help you to successfully position yourself for the next stage in your career. Generating specific work opportunities will take time and emotional investment; starting early will facilitate an effective transition.

## Summary

Actively engaging in a job search can take considerable time; typically, it also signals the beginning of a transition. Be sure not to leave this important stage to the last minute. Effective career management is ongoing, so it is always a good idea to be nurturing your network and generating potential leads.

Jasjit, introduced at the beginning of this chapter, will have a particularly challenging time generating leads as she is not yet certain about where she wants to live and work. Making those basic decisions needs to be her first step; just as it's impossible to navigate efficiently without a destination in mind, so it is essential to know where your career is headed before actively beginning the work search and interview process.

This chapter has provided strategies for generating concrete work opportunities, tips for how to network effectively, information about types of interviews and stages of the interview process, and an overview of the transition process. Use the questions provided to reflect on your learning from this chapter and take it to a deeper level through discussion.

## Questions for Reflection and Discussion

1. Jasjit is in the midst of multiple transitions: graduation, relocation, significant financial changes, and changing life roles as she builds a life after her divorce and adjusts to an "empty nest" as her children leave home one by one. Which of the transition models might be most helpful for Jasjit? What transitions are you going through? Which model or models are most helpful for you?

2. Generating specific job leads is likely to be challenging for Jasjit as she is currently unsure about where she wants to live. What recommendations would you give her for next steps post-graduation? How is Jasjit's situation similar to or different from yours? What can you do right now to generate specific job leads?

3. Everyone has some questions that they hope won't be asked in a job interview. What do you suppose Jasjit is dreading being asked? How might you help her prepare for those questions? What questions are you dreading and why? With a partner, brainstorm ways to effectively answer your problem questions.

## Additional Resources

Dumas, M. (2001). How to choose the best resume format. Retrieved July 30, 2009, from www.distinctiveweb.com/choose.htm. Choosing the appropriate resume format is made easy with this comprehensive resource. Information on targeted, inventory, chronological, functional, and combination resumes, complete with examples of each type of resume, is provided.

Quintessential Careers. (n.d.). Job interview questions database for job-seekers. Retrieved July 30, 2009, from www.quintcareers.com/interview_question_database/. A comprehensive database of traditional, behavioral, and non-traditional interview questions and answers.

Savara, S. (2009). Strategies for nurturing your professional network and professional relationships. Retrieved July 30, 2009, from http://sidsavara.com/personal-development/strategies-for-nurturing-your-professional-network-and-professional-relationships. This informative article provides statistics on the importance of networking as well as provides strategies for nurturing relationships with specific tips for how to apply the strategies in your own life.

# References

Amundson, N. E., & Borgen, W. A. (1987). Coping with unemployment: What helps and hinders. *Journal of Employment Counseling, 24*, 97–106.

Bridges, W. (2004). *Transitions: Making sense of life's changes* (2nd ed.). Cambridge, MA: Da Capo Press.

Krumboltz, J. D., & Levin, A. S. (2004). *Luck is no accident: Making the most of happenstance in your life and career.* Atascadero, CA: Impact Publishers.

Neault, R. A. (2002). Thriving in the new millennium: Career management in the changing world of work. *Canadian Journal of Career Development, 1*(1), 11–21.

"You've built your boat, now do what you must to stay afloat."

—Author Unknown

CHAPTER

# 12

# Career Flow Interrupted: Realizing Your Dreams in Challenging Times

## OBJECTIVES

This chapter focuses on how career flow can be interrupted by work and life events. By the end of this chapter, you will:

- Increase your awareness of some of the social and economic trends that might impact your career decision making

- Understand how to apply a "creating" stance to problems you face

- Learn how to cope with challenges such as unemployment, underemployment, mergers and downsizing, and other personal issues

## CASE STUDY

Edward is finishing his degree in psychology and has attained very good grades. During his school years, he worked in the summer in a youth program run by correctional services. When he thinks about career flow, he knows that he prefers working in a hectic environment (whitewater). He enjoys the challenge of multitasking and likes to be doing work that makes a difference. As he approaches the end of his training, he talks to his manager about future career options. There is every likelihood of a full-time job coming up in the fall, and he is obviously in a great position to qualify for this opportunity. It is suggested that he work part time during the summer and then when the job comes up, he can apply for it. He also has an opportunity to take a three-year contract position with an employment counseling agency. This position would start right after graduation.

Shutterstock

In assessing the situation, Edward decides that he really would like to wait for the correctional service position. During the break, he might be able to take that European holiday that he has been dreaming about. The only problem is lack of finances, but he can get a short-term loan and pay the money back when he starts working in the fall. Edward manages to get the funds for his trip and heads off on a three-month vacation. Unfortunately, toward the end of his trip, while visiting a small village in Norway, he receives an email message from his former manager advising him that there have been cutbacks and the position that he had counted on is no longer a possibility. This is obviously shocking news, but there is little Edward can do about it. He decides to finish his holiday and then restart the job search process.

## Social and Economic Trends

In exploring the topic of career flow, economic realities need to be considered. Uncertain times such as the economic tsunami in 2008 make it difficult to predict with any accuracy the specific job fields that will present the best opportunities upon graduation. However, this does not mean that there aren't certain social and economic trends that can be taken into account. Listed below are some of these trends and their implications:

1. Workers will generally need higher levels of critical thinking and skill training. This means that it is important to seek education where critical thinking and skill development are highlighted.

2. In positioning yourself during challenging economic times, it is helpful to think about social trends such as an aging population—increased need for health and social services; greater focus on environmental issues—find ways to be part of the emerging green economy, and consider security issues.

3. There will be more opportunities to work globally (multinational corporations). In order to work internationally, it is important to have some travel experiences, connect with people from other cultures, and learn other languages.

4. Communication and information technology will continue to play an important function. This does not mean that everyone needs to be a computer programmer, but there will be the expectation that you are able to use computers, word processing, cell phones, and so on.

5. Lifelong learning needs to be incorporated into your long-term plan. There is the expectation that you will keep learning while you are working. There also may be periods of time when you need to step outside of the workforce to acquire additional training.

6. There are no "safe" jobs where you can expect to spend your entire career. The idea of staying with one firm and working your way "up the ladder" no longer applies. Your focus needs to be on learning and improving your employability skills. When you have reached the limit of what a job can

offer you, it will be time to move on and look for other opportunities. Sometimes this will mean acquiring additional education to assist you in taking the next step.

7. In many situations, you will need to consider options other than the traditional full-time job with security. This means being willing to explore a portfolio career with elements of part-time work, contract work, and self-employment options.

8. Organizations are restructuring. As a result, often fewer numbers of middle management positions exist. Organizations also are impacted by mergers and downsizing. To stay afloat in the midst of turbulence, you need to be flexible and focus on your own need to keep growing your employability skills.

9. Employment opportunities will vary widely from region to region; to take advantage of emerging possibilities, you may need to consider moving to other parts of the country.

10. Despite all your best efforts, you may face periods of underemployment or even unemployment. There are some actions that can help you cope with these difficult situations. In such turbulence, it is important to remain true to yourself and your own personal and family needs. The choices you make should be grounded in personal health and integrity.

*Source:* Amundson, Harris-Bowlsbey, & Niles, 2009; Herr, 1999; Storey, 2000.

Hopefully, this list of trends has not generated any undue anxiety. It is meant to help you prepare for what lies ahead. Many people still operate on "yesterday's story." It is essential to understand that you need to become more proactive in directing your career development. Rather than just letting it happen, you need to have a vision of what you want to create for yourself and be prepared to play an active role in creating your own opportunities.

A starting point in directing your own career is to understand what you really enjoy (your passions) and how these passions translate into career flow experiences.

*Creative energy at work.*

istockphoto

With so much uncertainty all around, it is essential to have some form of anchor to rely on; otherwise, you will flip-flop from one situation to the other without regard for your personal needs, interests, and talents.

## The Problem with Problem Solving

As you contemplate social and labor market changes and your own situation, it is very easy to become apprehensive and anxious. In many ways, finding work has become much more challenging. So how does one approach the situation in a way that strengthens personal power and minimizes some of the anxiety associated with uncertainty? Perhaps some of the difficulty is the way in which problems are framed. Let's begin with a short exercise.

## *Creating versus Problem Solving*

ACTIVITY 12.1

1. Take a moment and think about a difficult problem in your life (it may be the issue of finding work after graduation) and how you need to problem solve the solution. What are your thoughts and feelings when you focus on a problem in this way?
   a. Thoughts
   b. Feelings

2. Now, take a deep breath, and shift to something you'd love to create— a dream you would love to make happen but haven't yet had the opportunity to realize. What thoughts and feelings are associated with this scenario?
   a. Thoughts
   b. Feelings

When we are in a problem-solving mode, many of us feel discouraged, overwhelmed, anxious, dispirited, hopeless, and so on. When in a creative mode, however, we feel energized, hopeful, excited about the possibilities, and ready to make it happen.

Robert Fritz (1989), in his classic book, *The Path of Least Resistance*, outlines the advantages of seeking a pathway with a heart. Bruce Elkin (2003) takes this further and illustrates how creativity is a more effective way of handling life challenges. He identifies the following flaws with a problem-solving approach and suggests that these flaws "prevent problem solving from consistently producing real and lasting results" (p. 62).

1. Problem solving often focuses on finding the right answer (a convergent approach). But what if the answer is more complex and does not lend itself easily to a single answer? In this scenario, a more creative approach allows for divergence and the flexibility one needs in solving problems.

2. When you are in a problem-solving mode, you often start from a weaker emotional position, that is, discouraged, anxious, or helpless. From a creative stance, more positive energy and excitement exists about what might be possible.

3. Problem solving often emphasizes temporary solutions that can be unsatis-factory in the long run. With a creative perspective, there is always a focus on what one ultimately wants to create and, even when there are challenges, these are viewed as temporary setbacks to the ultimate result.

4. When problem solving, you are usually generating actions and results that are viewed as either winning or losing. In a more complex world, it can be helpful to remove the either/or categories and view what is happening as part of a longer-term plan.

Elkin (2003) suggests that problem solving often leads to simplistic answers that don't fit well with our complex society. He also indicates that being creative is a more powerful motivating force than problem solving.

## Applying a Creating Approach

ACTIVITY 12.2

When it comes to viewing your own situation, take a moment to see if you can apply a more creative stance to the future you would like to create for yourself. Rather than being bombarded by negativity, start from a position of strength and creativity. Answer the following questions.

1. What matters to you and what type of life would you like to create for yourself?

_____

2. What needs to be done in order to get there—to make this a reality?

_____

3. What is the first step you need to take?

_____

Tip  *When you are facing a difficult situation, make a conscious effort to focus on your strengths. Think about a range of possibilities and try to be creative in developing strategies for success.*

## Coping with Challenges

### CASE STUDY CONTINUED

Edward returned to North America and restarted his job search. His friend's father owns a landscaping business, so that is one option that has emerged. He would make good money at this work and it would help him get out of debt. Another temporary position has opened up with correctional services; however, this job doesn't pay as well, it is with a different population (older workers), and it involves relocation to a small town several hours away from his current location. In addition, the job does not have the same energy (whitewater) level that was part of his previous experience.

Even if you adopt a creating stance toward building your career, challenges such as interruptions in career flow still may occur. In this section, we explore some of these challenges and offer some suggestions of ways to overcome the barriers.

### Unemployment

While it would be great to imagine that you will not face periods of unemployment, the reality is that many people (even those with a good education) might find themselves having to cope with this challenge. So, what is known about this barrier? Borgen, Hatch, and Amundson (1990), in a study of the experience of unemployment for college graduates, reported that in the initial stage, many of the students were happy to be finished with school and to have the free time to enjoy themselves. There was graduation, perhaps some travel, and general relaxation. The challenge became more prominent after a few months when some friends went back to school or found work. Financial pressure started to become a significant factor and self-confidence began to dissipate. People devalued their education and negatively viewed their prospects for the future. Job searches became more focused, but the negative results served to drag them down further. The unemployment experience had a negative emotional impact (Linnehan & Blau, 1998). According to Borgen and Amundson (1987), many people undergo a negative roller coaster experience. There might be some good prospects and this pulls a person up, but when it doesn't work out a rapid downward swing takes place and further discouragement sets in. This experience incorporates aspects of loss and burnout reactions.

People who have gone through unemployment have some good suggestions about how to cope (Amundson & Borgen, 1987). First, it is important to recognize that the cause of the challenge can be attributed in most cases to

*Sometimes there are challenges to be faced.*

istockphoto

the state of the labor market. It is essential to separate out personal responsibility from external causes. Second, in a tense situation you may find yourself having more interpersonal difficulties with friends and family. It is important to talk about your feelings and keep people informed and involved in the job search process. Rather than cutting people off, find ways to engage them in positive conversation. As a third strategy, you might find it helpful to connect with an employment counselor and get involved in a job search support group, where you will learn more effective job search strategies and have more opportunities for mutually supportive relationships. Fourth, stay active in all aspects of life. Seek volunteer experiences and get involved in hobbies and leisure pursuits. By being active, you increase your chances of making connections and you establish other outlets for involvement. Looking for work requires ongoing effort, but it also is stressful and you need to have other positive activities in your life. As a fifth strategy, consider options such as retraining or taking a survival job (perhaps part-time or temporary work). Lastly, if the bills keep piling up, it may be helpful to seek some financial counseling.

## Underemployment

There are many ways of becoming underemployed. Sometimes it is a matter of not valuing the skills you have acquired and, as a result, settling for work that is not very challenging. There can also be family dynamics that serve to undermine talents and abilities. For some college graduates, it is the lack of immediate employment prospects and the need to get something in place to meet financial obligations and to avoid unemployment.

There is nothing inherently wrong with underemployment. Depending on life circumstances, there are times when we need to find work that does not fully utilize our skills. The challenge for most is to not get trapped into this type of work situation on a long-term basis. Many start out taking a job just to have something in place and then, with time, redefine their lives so that what started out as short-term work becomes their regular job. With the passage of time, it becomes less likely that they will ever have the opportunity to use their training.

The major issue with underemployment is that we tend to give up on our dreams. The longer we are away from our skill training, the more likely the skills will become obsolete. Lack of relevant work experience also becomes an issue and contributes to the failure to continue working in a field of interest.

For some, being underemployed creates emotional reactions similar to unemployment (Borgen, Amundson, & Harder, 1988)—feelings of discouragement and distress coupled with a general lack of meaning and purpose in life. Being cut off from interests and abilities can have a significant negative psychological impact.

Perhaps the best way of dealing with underemployment is to always keep in mind your long-term objectives. While some jobs may serve short-term needs, it is important to be ready to shift the focus back to the original goal as soon as possible (or create new goals). There are also times when we need to think carefully about available work options. Sometimes it is a better choice to accept a position that pays less but offers more relevant experience and opportunities for further learning (Larkin, LaPort, & Pines, 2007). If you are engaged in activities where there are more opportunities for flow, you likely will do better work and, as a result, have the opportunity to get good references from supervisors and managers.

## Work Challenges through Mergers and Downsizing

Finding that initial great job is only a starting point and, for some people, changes can occur quite quickly through organizational mergers and downsizing. If you have little seniority, then there can be prolonged periods of uncertainty while organizations restructure themselves. Even if you don't lose your job, there can be significant changes to the quality of working life. Amundson, Borgen, Jordan, and Erlebach (2004) explored some of these experiences for survivors of organizational downsizing. What stood out in this research was the emotional upheaval during a time of downsizing. Some of this turbulence negatively impacted relationships with coworkers and managers and had the potential to be a stressful factor on the homefront. In some instances, a downsized environment created certain work challenges—an overload of work, lack of training for the work that needed to be done, and a lack of feedback and supervision. At a personal level, morale was often impacted by the lack of personal validation and poor communication.

Of course, this downsizing experience is not a uniformly negative experience. There also are opportunities to form new relationships, to extend skills, and to build closer relationships with coworkers, managers, and family members. In order to successfully navigate through this type of experience, it is essential to remain open to new experiences, to accept uncertainty as part of the situation, and to make choices based on what you know about yourself and your own capacity. There are times when it is just a matter of weathering a storm and other situations when you need to look elsewhere for new possibilities. Having a clear vision about what you would like to achieve in your work can help you with your decision making.

## Life Challenges

Stress can enter working life in many ways: healthcare issues for yourself, family, or friends; issues with the criminal justice system; and financial or economic problems. All of these issues carry over into the workplace (Hobson, Delunas, & Kesic, 2001) and, in many instances, more than one of these stressors can be operative at the same time.

In dealing with these stressors, it is important to seek support from others and, when necessary, to seek professional help. The resolution of personal issues plays an important part in ensuring work satisfaction.

# CASE STUDY CONCLUDED

Edward decided to take the job with correctional services, even though it did not pay as well. He wanted the experience and was willing to accept a lower wage.

Initially, he was frustrated by the lack of intensity in the new position but kept working hard and took advantage of every opportunity to acquire some additional education. Eventually, a more interesting and better-paying position opened up, and he was selected for the position.

Tip     *Even when there are interruptions in career flow, if you keep working at it (with your vision in mind), you will be better able to take advantage of emerging opportunities.*

## Summary

These are uncertain times. Unexpected challenges will appear, and problems will need to be faced. In dealing with these issues, it is helpful to adopt a "creating" stance. With this approach, there is the possibility of attaining greater energy and enthusiasm for the task at hand and learning to think broadly about possible solutions.

In preparing for a more turbulent social and economic situation, you may face challenges such as unemployment, underemployment, mergers and downsizing, and personal life issues. While these challenges present some real life/career barriers, they are not insurmountable. Much of the information from this book can be useful when dealing with such challenges.

## Questions for Reflection and Discussion

1. What are your thoughts about how Edward handled his situation? In responding to this question, think about some current social and economic trends.

2. Can you apply some of these trends to your situation?

3. How would adopting a "creating" approach to your career search change the way you think and feel about the process?

## References

Amundson, N. E., & Borgen, W. A. (1987). *At the controls: Charting your course through unemployment.* Toronto: Nelson Canada.

Amundson, N. E., Borgen, W. A., Jordan, S., & Erlebach, A. C. (2004). Survivors of downsizing: Helpful and hindering experiences. *The Career Development Quarterly, 52,* 256–271.

Amundson, N. E., Harris-Bowlsbey, J., & Niles, S. G. (2009). *Essential elements of career counseling: Processes and techniques* (2nd ed.). Upper Saddle River, NJ: Pearson.

Borgen, W. A., & Amundson, N. E. (1987). The dynamics of unemployment. *Journal of Counseling and Development, 66,* 180–184.

Borgen, W. A., Amundson, N. E., & Harder, H. G. (1988). The experience of underemployment. *Journal of Employment Counseling, 25,* 149–159.

Borgen, W. A., Hatch, W. E., & Amundson, N. E. (1990). The experience of unemployment for university graduates: An exploratory study. *Journal of Employment Counseling, 27,* 104–112.

Elkin, B. (2003). *Simplicity and success: Creating the life you long for.* Victoria, BC: Trafford.

Fritz, R. (1989). *The path of least resistance: Learning to become the creative force in your own life.* New York: Fawcett Columbine.

Herr, E. L. (1999). *Counseling in a dynamic society: Contexts & practices for the 21st century.* Alexandria, VA: American Counseling Association.

Hobson, C. J., Delunas, L., & Kesic, D. (2001). Compelling evidence of the need for corporate work/life balance initiatives: Results from a national survey of stressful life-events. *Journal of Employment Counseling, 38,* 38–44.

Larkin, J. E., LaPort, K. A., & Pines, H. A. (2007). Job choice and career relevance for today's college students. *Journal of Employment Counseling, 44,* 86–94.

Linnehan, F., & Blau, G. (1998). Exploring the emotional side of job search behavior for younger workforce entrants. *Journal of Employment Counseling, 35,* 98–113.

Storey, J. (2000). 'Fracture lines' in the career environment. In A. Collins & R. Young (Eds.), *The future of career* (pp. 21–36). Cambridge: Cambridge University Press.

# Notes

**"** Difficulties are meant to rouse, not discourage. The human spirit is to grow strong by conflict. **"**

—*William Ellery Channing*

# 13

# Whitewater and Stillwater Career Flow Experiences

## OBJECTIVES

This chapter focuses on whitewater and stillwater career flow experiences. After this chapter, you will be able to:

- Define "whitewater" career flow experiences
- Use strategies for coping effectively with whitewater career flow experiences
- Define "stillwater" career flow experiences
- Use strategies for coping effectively with stillwater career flow experiences

## CASE STUDY

Robert is the newly elected president of the student government association at his college. He is a fairly effective leader overall, but there are times when he seems to really "hit the panic button." When the demands of his presidency run high, he gets very stressed out. Often, he will snap at those he works with, and he has even been known to scream at others. His anger in these moments scares those around him. He clearly gets overwhelmed with all the tasks he feels he must complete. Rarely does he ask others for help or take time out to prioritize his tasks.

Other times, when the activity level is low, Robert procrastinates. It is almost as though he does a complete 180-degree turn. He seems relaxed and laid back in these moments. He encourages others to not worry about things when the demands are few. He reminds those around him how important it is to "smell the roses." Many times, this approach leads Robert to fall behind on his tasks. Then, as the deadlines near, he becomes overly stressed again. To others, it seems like he is engaged in a vicious cycle of either overreacting or underreacting. Lately, Robert has begun noticing his tendencies and has wondered what he can do to address things more effectively.

This chapter focuses on two dimensions of career flow: whitewater and stillwater. It is very likely that your current life experience contains both dimensions, and it is a certainty that both dimensions will be part of your future work experience. So, because these experiences cannot be avoided altogether, the key is to learn how to manage each dimension of your career flow effectively. Clearly, Robert is struggling with both. It is important to understand whitewater and stillwater career flow experiences and to learn what can be done to manage them as effectively as possible.

## Defining Whitewater Career Flow Experiences

The term *whitewater* is appropriate for describing high-demand periods in your career because these experiences are similar to the whitewater rapids you can encounter in a journey down a river. Skilled whitewater rafters tend to love the thrill they experience while they are in the midst of rapid running currents. They know that the river's whitewater will challenge their skills, offering exhilaration and excitement. They have confidence because they have developed the skills required for reading and navigating the whitewater effectively. The most experienced rafters are always well prepared for coping with the whitewater they encounter. They know how to react when the river presents various challenges. They use their skills in conjunction with the currents to guide the raft safely through the water. They know their limits and how to manage their raft so they minimize the likelihood of the whitewater exceeding their limits.

Stay in the whitewater too long, however, and even the most accomplished rafter will become exhausted. In such instances, knowing how to paddle out of the rapids is an important skill. Sometimes there is a fine line between feeling exhilarated and feeling overwhelmed. Some rafters seek out rivers that contain the most challenging whitewater while others prefer staying in calmer currents. Even currents that tend to be calm can contain some whitewater, however.

*Whitewater can be exhilarating when you have the skills to conquer the challenges.*

istockphoto

There are similarities between the experience of rafters encountering whitewater and your career development.

You will, in your work and in your education, occasionally feel as if you are in the whitewater currents. The demands will be high and constant. The challenges will be substantial. In some occupations (e.g., police officer), these challenges can occur frequently. In other occupations (e.g., accountant), they may occur primarily at specific periods that are fairly predictable (e.g., during tax season). The key is to develop the skills necessary for recognizing and managing these stressful times when they arise. The good news is that you can begin to develop these skills now and put them to use in your college career so that when you encounter whitewater experiences in your future career, you will be able to cope with them effectively.

## A Stressful Activity

ACTIVITY 13.1    Consider how you handle stressful situations and respond to each of the following questions:

- How do you deal with stressful experiences when you encounter them?

- Do you enjoy it when you encounter high demands on your time?

- What do you not like about stressful experiences?

- Identify two or three emotions you tend to have when you encounter stressful experiences.

- How could you handle these times more effectively?

As a college student, your times of whitewater are fairly predictable. Some rather swift currents occur at the beginning of each academic semester; at mid-semester, those currents become even more rapid; finally, at the end of each semester, you experience the rapids in full force as you encounter final exams and other end-of-semester assignments. These higher stress times provide you with the opportunity to begin using important and lifelong self-management skills that will help you navigate the rapids of your academic experience effectively. These same skills become essential as you move into your career beyond college.

Tip    *Whitewater can be exhilarating or overwhelming. How you choose to handle it makes all the difference.*

## Strategies for Managing Whitewater Career Flow Experiences

You can begin practicing several important strategies right now to manage the whitewater or high demands you experience. For example, it is key that you practice good self-care habits. Regular exercise such as walking, biking, running, lifting weights, yoga, and so on provides a buffer against excessive stress. Your exercise routine does not need to resemble an Olympic athlete's training schedule, but it should be consistent. Thirty to forty minutes of exercise daily can provide tremendous benefits to you at all times but especially during those times when you are faced with many demands. Exercise will help you relax, stay positive, keep alert, and ward off some illnesses. Exercising with a friend or group of friends adds a dimension of social support that is also essential for managing the demands of college and work life. This is an important strategy and calls on the sage advice that "an ounce of prevention is worth a pound of cure."

Social support may be the most important strategy you can use for coping with stressful times. Research from social psychology is helpful here. What people seem to find most useful in coping with stress is not simply the opportunity to interact with others, although that is important. Rather, people find it especially helpful to interact with others who are experiencing similar challenges. For example, if you are confused about selecting a college major, then you will find it very helpful to find opportunities to interact with others experiencing this same challenge. Most university career centers provide such opportunities for students. Career planning courses, career decision-making groups, major-selection workshops, and similar activities are helpful ways to receive social support regarding the task of making career and educational choices. What specific benefits do these activities offer? First, you will find out that there are many other students (maybe even the majority of students at your college) who are not certain about their educational and career choices. This helps you to recognize that uncertainty is very normal. Moreover, as you interact with others who are undecided, you will find that they will share their experiences as to what has and what has not been helpful to them in their own efforts to make choices. This information may be helpful to you regarding what to consider trying and what to avoid experiencing in your own decision-making

*The support of others can make all the difference.*

istockphoto

process. When career decision-making classes or groups are led by a career professional, you will also receive important information and tips regarding how to go about the decision-making process systematically. Like other tasks you encounter in life, career and educational decision making involve specific skills and knowledge areas you can learn and practice. A good instructor will help you learn these.

Tip    *Support from others can help you cope with substantial challenges in your career.*

Another essential skill, especially when you experience excessive demands on your time, is time management. A key component of time management is the ability to prioritize activities into categories: (1) those you are required to complete immediately, (2) those you are required to complete but not immediately, and (3) optional activities. With optional activities, decide which ones you could immediately eliminate from your "to do" list by deciding not to do them at all and which ones you choose to do but can do at a later time. The point here is that sometimes we get caught up with multiple assignments and do not approach completing them systematically. When you begin to feel overwhelmed with demands on your time, initiate this sorting process.

Once you have listed the activities according to their category, identify the activity you will focus on first. Then, establish a list of goals for the week ahead. Write these down and refer to them throughout the week. Do this with each of the activities included in your "complete immediately" category. If you have a tendency toward procrastination, then you may find it most useful to first focus on completing the easiest task within this category. This will allow you to experience some success and generate some momentum toward completing subsequent tasks in this category. Using this approach to sort through your to do list will help you take control over the demands on your time.

Monitoring your thoughts is also a strategy you can use when you are confronted with whitewater experiences in your career. For example, many of us engage in what is referred to as *catastrophizing* when we encounter a whitewater experience. In a way similar to Robert in our case example, we "hit the panic button." In other words, our thoughts become focused on worst-case scenarios such as: "If I don't complete this task perfectly, I will be a complete failure," "If I don't get this right, she will decide I am stupid," or "If I don't do a great job on this speech, people will laugh at me and decide not to be my friend anymore." When you are panicking about at task that needs to be completed, most likely you are catastrophizing.

## *Controlling Catastrophizing*

ACTIVITY 13.2    To gain control over catastrophizing, first pay attention to the emotional experience or the feelings you have when you encounter a challenging task or multiple challenging tasks. Think about a specific instance when this occurred recently for you. Close your eyes and try to remember the experience.

*(continued)*

**ACTIVITY 13.2**
(continued)

- What happened and how did you feel?

- Can you locate the feeling within your body? (Some people notice that they have queasiness in their stomach or tightness in their shoulders.)

- What other reactions do you have? Do you eat more or eat less food? Do you have trouble sleeping?

- Try to identify your specific reactions when you encounter whitewater experiences.

Now, try to identify any thoughts you might have had related to these experiences (e.g., "I have to be perfect," "I'll never be good enough," "If I fail, it will be proof that I'm a failure"). Even if you have trouble identifying specific thoughts, try to guess at what you might be thinking in these instances (thoughts cause feelings, so if you have identified uncomfortable feelings, there is a good chance you have engaged in negative thinking).

- List the thought(s):

To counteract the effects of catastrophizing, it is important to challenge or dispute the negative thought. For example, if you thought "I will be a failure if I do not complete this assignment perfectly," you could revise this to "I will do the best I can with this assignment and if it isn't perfect, that is okay because no one is perfect." Or, if you had a thought similar to "I cannot change my major because it is a failure if I change my plans," you could challenge this by acknowledging the following: "Changing my plans is not failing; it is an acknowledgment of the fact that I have learned more information about myself and my options and I am deciding to choose an option that fits me better than my current plans. Changing is a positive response to new information I have acquired."

- Propose a more constructive alternative to the negative thought you identified.

It is important that whenever you notice the negative feelings or reactions you identified above that you consider the possibility that you may have told yourself negative or catastrophizing thoughts. When you notice this, consider what the thoughts may have been and challenge them with more constructive possibilities. This strategy takes practice, but over time it can change your entire approach to challenges you encounter.

Finally, another strategy many people find useful for managing stressful or whitewater experiences is the consistent practice of meditation. For many people, this activity is invaluable for coping with a hectic life. Meditation provides opportunities for slowing down. It allows you to become less attached to your thoughts as you ground your activities in areas that accurately reflect your core values. No single meditation style seems to have a corner on the market relative to effectiveness. Whether you practice the "relaxation response" (which usually involves counting your breaths), transcendental meditation (silently repeating a sacred word or phrase), or any other of the myriad forms of meditation, engaging in meditation for 10–20 minutes twice a day seems to have very positive physical and psychological benefits. You will find that you are less influenced by others and by the demands others place on you. You will react to situations in a more levelheaded way and maintain a calm perspective more frequently than during times when you do not meditate. You will certainly cope with the whitewater moments of your career more effectively.

As you move out of the whitewater periods in your education and work, there is the tendency to relax your attention to self-care activities. It often feels like they are less necessary when the demands subside. The truth is, however, that these strategies are important to follow at all times. Practicing them regularly will have positive benefits for you.

## Robert's Whitewater

**ACTIVITY 13.3**     Consider Robert's whitewater experiences.

- How does he currently handle these?

_____

- What steps could he take to handle these more effectively?

_____

- How do you handle whitewater experiences?

_____

- Think about a time in the recent past when you felt overwhelmed.

_____

- What did you do?

_____

- How well did your strategy work?

_____

- What are two steps you could take to handle these experiences more effectively in the future?

_____

## Defining Stillwater Career Flow Experiences

*Stillwater experiences help you regroup and re-energize.*

The opposite of whitewater is stillwater. On a river, stillwater currents are, obviously, still. If a rafter wants to move forward when in stillwater, the rafter has to paddle constantly and exert force to overcome inertia. Moving forward only occurs with consistent and intentional effort. If the stillwater follows a period of whitewater, then the rafter may choose to use the stillwater to regroup, relax, and rest. The stillwater can be a welcome respite from the rapid currents. Stay too long in the stillwater, however, and most people become bored. The stillwater becomes stagnant.

Your career will undoubtedly contain stillwater moments. As with rafting, the stillwaters can offer valuable times to rest, regroup, and, if necessary, redirect your career-related activities. Knowing how long to tolerate the stillwater is important. If you stay for too long in a situation that does not challenge your skills, your skills will grow weaker and, in today's world of work, perhaps even irrelevant. You become, in essence, too comfortable being comfortable with your expertise, knowledge, and skills. When you become too comfortable with what you have already done (resting on your laurels so to speak), you become less marketable rather quickly. For example, computer skills that are necessary today did not even exist one year ago. If you have not kept up, you have fallen behind, and that means you are less marketable in today's labor market.

Thus, the stillwater presents its own challenges. Knowing how long to stay in situations that do not require you to grow or present you with challenges is essential. Understanding when it is time to "paddle out of the stillwater" is crucial. Paddling out often requires you to know how to seek out challenges, acquire growth experiences, and identify new learning opportunities and skills that offer movement out of the stillwater. Acquiring new knowledge and skills can help you become innovative in your career, thereby becoming more valuable to your employer.

In today's world of work, lifelong learning is essential, so developing your comfort with learning new skills is a key factor in becoming a successful employee. A willingness to move beyond your comfort zone is an expectation of workers today. You can begin to develop this now by taking steps to learn new skills via courses, independent reading, volunteering, extracurricular activities, and so on.

## Strategies for Coping with Stillwater Career Flow Experiences

Managing stillwater experiences effectively involves using the 4 Rs: reflecting, regrouping, re-energizing, and redirecting. When you encounter stillwater experiences, you may initially find them enjoyable; indeed, the "down times" are necessary. Using them wisely involves being intentional about reflecting on your life and work. Ongoing self-reflection is crucial to maintaining self-clarity. Considering what you enjoy and what you do not enjoy about your career situation is important. Just like people must routinely go to the dentist for check-ups, you must routinely take time to check in as to what is working for you and what is not. Doing a full assessment of your current situation is critical to managing your career effectively, and the stillwater moments provide an excellent opportunity for this.

## Stillwater Reflection

ACTIVITY 13.4      Consider the questions posed in the previous paragraph and respond to the following:

- What skills would you like to develop?

- Which (if any) of your core values are you not able to express in your current situation?

- Is there a passion you are not able to express in your current situation?

- Is there an aspect to your current situation you find very unappealing (perhaps even despicable)?

After you complete this activity, ask yourself whether there are any actions you can take to improve your current situation. Try to choose one activity—learning a new hobby, volunteering, taking more time for yourself, doing an activity with a friend, and so on—that would allow you to improve things.

Unfortunately, many of us think that engaging in such reflection is not necessary after a certain point in our career development. Nothing could be further from the truth! A basic premise of career development is that we continue to develop throughout our lives. New experiences often result in new insights, new behaviors, and new goals. When we act as if our development is frozen in time, we ignore one of the most basic facts. When we choose to ignore our ongoing self-development, we do so at our own peril. This approach to living leads to a level of discontent that at first may be subtle but over time becomes almost impossible to deny. Thus, when we live as if we do not change, we do great injury to ourselves. Over time, we may develop substance abuse behaviors, physical ailments, and/or psychological disorders. So, it makes good sense to minimize these occurrences! Engaging in regular and ongoing reflection and assessment about your current level of career satisfaction is one strategy for maximizing opportunities for enhanced happiness and minimizing the negative effects of living an unsatisfying life. Stillwater experiences provide excellent opportunities for such reflection.

Moreover, even if you do not continue to evolve over time as you live your life, there is overwhelming evidence that the world of work does not stay the same. Jobs exist today that did not exist one year ago—and vice versa. New technologies make the same job different from one year ago. To keep up with such changes in the world of work, you must engage in lifelong learning. The dynamic interaction between ongoing self-development and ongoing developments in the world of work make asking the questions related to reflection an ongoing requirement for effective career self-management.

Tip    *Reflecting provides the opportunity for regrouping and redirecting. Practice it on a regular basis.*

Stillwater experiences also offer opportunities for regrouping and redirecting. Similar to a sporting event in which one team takes a timeout, regrouping allows you to consider what you need to do next in your career to respond most effectively to your current situation. Put simply, regrouping allows you to ask how things are going in your career (i.e., reflecting) and then decide on appropriate steps to take next. As you consider next steps, it is useful to clarify the degree to which you may need to redirect your time and energy. Often, you will decide to stay the course. Other times, however, you may identify minor changes that need to be made in your career. Still other times, you may determine that major changes must be made. Sometimes, the changes are immediate; other times, they may be changes you need to prepare for over time. Redirecting, therefore, at all times, involves developing a plan for the future. However, because you continue to develop as you live your life and because the world of work continues to develop, any plans you make must remain open to revision as you continue to engage in reflection—especially during the stillwater moments in your career development.

The entire process of reflecting, regrouping, and redirecting creates new energy as you move forward in your career development. When you become intentional about ensuring that your career provides the greatest opportunities for expressing key aspects of who you are, then you naturally become re-energized. In a sense, you become like the rafter who moves effortlessly down the river, enjoying the experience to the utmost. It is important for you to note when you have these sorts of experiences in your life. Identify what the feeling is like. Clarify how it feels as compared to when your activities are not as fully aligned with what you like, value, and enjoy.

Noting the feeling of this sort of experience is important for two reasons. First, it reinforces the importance of reflecting, regrouping, and redirecting. Second, it helps you to identify when your activities may be out of alignment with key aspects of your personality. Identifying when the latter is occurring should help to remind you of the need to reflect, regroup, and redirect so that you can become re-energized once again. Remember that these are continual processes. When you embrace this fact, you become a more effective manager of your own career development. Although the 4 Rs strategy can be used at any time to help you in your career, the stillwater experiences provide you with an excellent opportunity for using them to get back on track in your career.

## Summary

All people experience whitewater and stillwater moments in their career development. Thus, the question becomes whether you have developed the skills for identifying and addressing them when they occur. With practice, you can become more effective at coping with these career flow challenges. By beginning to develop these strategies now, in your role as a student, you will be proficient at them as you advance in your career.

## Questions for Reflection and Discussion

1. Consider the case study of Robert provided at the beginning of this chapter. How effective is Robert at dealing with whitewater and stillwater career flow experiences? If you were advising him as to how he might increase his skills for addressing these career flow challenges, what would you recommend?

2. Identify two things you enjoy about whitewater and stillwater career flow experiences. Now address two things you dislike about whitewater and stillwater. Are there any skills you can develop to address the things you do not like about these dimensions of your career flow?

3. Identify one stress management strategy you could learn in the next month. Commit to practicing this strategy over this time period.

## Additional Resources

Use the following websites to learn more about stress management techniques:
www.mindtools.com/smpage.html
www.medicinenet.com/stress_management_techniques/article.html
www.hypnos.info/book2/book2.html

A few books about stress management:
*The Everything Stress Management Book: Practical Ways to Relax, Be Healthy, and Maintain Your Sanity* by Eve Adamson
*7 Simple Steps to Unclutter Your Life* by Donna Smallin
*Naked* by David Sedaris

A longer list of stress management books:
www.books4selfhelp.com/recommended-most.htm#stress

66 The greatest thing by far is to be a master of metaphor. 99

—*Aristotle*

# 14

# Expanding the Career Flow Metaphor

## OBJECTIVES

This chapter is designed to include other career–life metaphors. By the end of this chapter, you will be able to:

- Use a journey metaphor to understand and make changes to your career–life process
- View your life/career using the image of a book
- Use a wide variety of other perspectives to understand your career–life process
- Incorporate a legacy perspective

## CASE STUDY

Aaron has grown up loving the outdoors and working with his hands. As a small boy, he would walk behind his father with his own toy lawnmower when the lawn was cut. In a career flow exercise in 12th grade, he clearly articulated a desire to work in landscaping and with trees.

Aaron has been accepted into a horticulture program and is excited about the future that lies in front of him. However, after a few weeks in the program, he is becoming very disillusioned. Many of the other students are older, and he did not count on having to learn all the Latin names for the plants. Rather than working outside with his hands, he is required to take classes that he feels are not very interesting. He comes to see a career counselor looking for a change, stating that he just doesn't seem to fit in this program. The program literature looked promising, but the reality is very different from his expectations.

As part of the career counseling Aaron received, he was encouraged to view his experience in the horticultural program as a journey. At the moment, he was experiencing some difficult challenges (bumps in the road), but there would be other times when things would go more smoothly. There also was a focus on some of the ways in which he could be more proactive about his experience. For example, at lunch he was leaving the site and eating lunch in his truck. As a result, he was not getting to know some of the other students. Even if they were a bit older, the relationships might still be interesting.

Aaron did change his view of the situation, and he enacted some of the suggested coping strategies. After a short period of time, the program became more practical and he became fully engaged. Even the learning of Latin names for plants became somewhat interesting. Today, Aaron is working successfully in the field as a landscaper and arborist.

Many metaphors can be applied to a person's career, and it is our position that *career flow* is one of the most helpful metaphors for understanding and working with career development issues. Hopefully, as you have gone through this book, you have found many new insights about your career.

There is value, however, in considering some of these other metaphors and perspectives. With this in mind, this final chapter moves beyond the career flow metaphor and opens up the career exploration process to other perspectives. This expansion encourages a broader range of creativity.

*The journey continues.*

Shutterstock

## Career as a Journey

One of the most popular career metaphors is the *journey*. Career flow can be part of this journey, but many other aspects need to be considered as part of the general movement through time and space (the journey).

## *Viewing Your Career as a Journey*

**ACTIVITY 14.1**    How would you describe your career journey up to this point in time? As you consider this, think about the way the path may have gone up and down, the peaks and the valleys. Think also about the general direction of the path. Has it been in a straight line, or have you been traveling back and forth? Another piece of this image might be the speed at which you are traveling. Are you moving as fast as you would like, or have you been stalled in some of your movements? As a final part of this picture, what do you see lying ahead? Can you extend the journey in some way and point to some possibilities? Using these general guidelines as a framework, describe your story—it can often be helpful to share.

1. Peaks and valleys

   _____

   _____

2. Direction

   _____

   _____

3. Speed and momentum

   _____

   _____

4. Future developments

   _____

   _____

## *Drawing the Journey Metaphor*

ACTIVITY 14.2        Sometimes, when using the journey metaphor, it is not enough to just put it into words. If you are a visual type of person, try to create and draw a depiction of what this metaphor might look like. Even if you aren't a great artist, try to draw something that would reflect your experience:

## *Changing the Visual Image*

ACTIVITY 14.3        Look closely at the image you have drawn. Are there any ways you can change the image to make it more positive? What would you need to do to change what you have drawn?

_____

_____

_____

_____

Sometimes, the first step is just changing the images we have about our experiences. With a new image, you can start to think practically about what would need to be done. Suppose your journey has moved in many different directions. What would it take to straighten the path a little? Specify what type of planning, support, and resources you would need.

Planning:

_____

_____

_____

Support:

_____

_____

_____

Resources:

_____

_____

_____

## Your Life as a Book

In many ways, we can look at our lives as stories that are unfolding. Stories can go in many directions, but there is usually a sense of pulling the story together into a coherent whole. In representing our life in this way, the metaphor of the book comes to mind. In this segment, we would like you to view your career–life story (including your career and life patterns) as a book.

*The story is being written.*

## Describing Your Life as a Book

ACTIVITY 14.4

**STEP 1**

Consider your life as if it were a book and give your book (i.e., your life) a title.

Title: _____

**STEP 2**

Divide your book (i.e., your life) into chapters and give each chapter of your life a title.

_____

_____

_____

**STEP 3**

List three lessons learned from living each of the chapters of your life.

_____

_____

_____

**STEP 4**

Think about your future and identify the name of the chapter(s) that you have yet to live but must live for your book (i.e., your life) to be complete.

_____

_____

_____

**STEP 5**

List three things you must do (e.g., learn new skills, let go of certain situations, make changes in how you spend your time) to increase the probability that you will live the chapter you identified in Step 4.

_____

_____

_____

It can be helpful to report this information using a small booklet format. In other words, actually create a small book with your life as the focus. The outside cover will display the title. Also think about the colors and designs that you might use on the cover. As you open the book, the table of contents lists chapter titles and brief descriptors under each one; this is where you would include some of the lessons learned. The chapters listed will include those already lived and those still to be written. With the future-oriented chapters, you will need to focus on what needs to happen to realize the goals that you have set for yourself. In defining your chapters, try to put events into unique configurations that capture meaningful events in your life. This is an opportunity to reflect broadly on your life and to use some creativity. For example, one student used the titles of Beatles songs as inspiration for the chapters he was outlining.

This activity allows you to use the past to enlighten the present and guide your future. The title of your book summarizes your life story. It provides a window into the major losses, obstacles, and achievements you have experienced in your life. The chapters of your life highlight the ways in which your priorities have evolved across time. They provide "tracks" that allow you to trace the ways in which you have made meaning out of your life experiences. As you review your chapter titles and lessons, you may notice patterns or themes playing out throughout your life. A way to identify the themes is to reflect on the titles and lessons learned. Ask yourself what they have in common and how they may be connected to each other. In doing this, you may find it helpful to identify the values embedded in your activities or reflected in your lessons learned. Your future chapter provides a sense of direction. It allows you to identify a goal and then to begin planning how you can achieve this goal.

## Other Metaphors and Perspectives

There are, of course, many other metaphors and perspectives that could be used to describe your life and career. The advantage of viewing yourself in other ways is that your creativity and flexibility increase as you consider these additional perspectives. In the following exercise, a range of perspectives is provided to encourage further reflection.

### *Expanding Your Perspective*

ACTIVITY 14.5    Take some time to systematically go through this list and, with each image, write down some of the new elements that occur as you view your life/career through the various images. If you can't think of anything for a particular item, just set it aside and keep going through the list. At the end, you may want to add some other images. Again, the focus here is on expanding creativity and flexibility by thinking about yourself using many different perspectives.

- **Anomaly**—a deviation or departure from the usual way things are done

_____

- **Breakthrough**—a major achievement or success that permits further progress

_____

- **Calling**—a strong inner urge or prompting; a strong attraction or appeal toward a given activity or environment

_____

- **Dance**—a creative physical expression; following a rhythm

_____

- **Esthetic**—something of beauty or good taste

_____

- **Fit**—to be properly in place

_____

- **Garden**—a plot of ground where plants are cultivated

_____

- **Handicraft**—creatively using skill to produce a useful product

_____

- **Inheritance**—any attribute or possession that comes from significant others

_____

- **Jungle**—land overgrown with tangled trees and vegetation

_____

- **Kaleidoscope**—a series of changing phases or events; constantly changing patterns

_____

- **Ladder**—a device for climbing to a higher place

_____

- **Management**—creating order and structure

_____

- **Networking**—connections with others

_____

- **Opportunity**—a favorable or advantageous circumstance

_____

- **Puzzle**—pieces of a picture to be formed

_____

- **Quest**—the act of seeking or pursuing something; a search

_____

- **Relationships**—the connection between people related to or having dealings with one another

_____

- **Stages**—a level, degree, or period of time in the course of a process

_____

*(continued)*

**ACTIVITY 14.5**
(continued)

- **Theater**—a place that is the setting for dramatic events

  _____

- **Uncertainty**—being unsure or doubtful

  _____

- **Venture**—an undertaking that is daring or of uncertain outcome

  _____

- **Wellness**—a condition of good physical and mental health

  _____

- **Exposition**—a showcase of talent

  _____

- **Yoke**—something that is put on in order to enable a task

  _____

- **Zenith**—highest point; time or place of greatest power or prosperity or happiness

  _____

- **Other Images**

  _____

## Your Legacy

As one final metaphor, it might be interesting to think ahead to the end of life and consider what kind of legacy you would like to leave behind based on the work and the life you have lived. Our actions and our attitudes influence others, and sometimes it is interesting to think about what types of stories (your legacy) you would like to have told about you at the end of your journey.

This is probably one of the most challenging metaphors to consider. If you are having trouble thinking about your own story, think about someone you know and admire. What kind of legacy are they leaving? What are the stories you will tell about their actions and attitudes?

*Stories are being told.*

Shutterstock

## *Creating a Legacy*

ACTIVITY 14.6          What type of legacy would you like to leave behind?

_____

_____

_____

_____

_____

Even if you can formulate your legacy at this point, it is important to recognize that in everything you do, you are leaving a story behind. This story can be uplifting and powerful, or it can lack meaning and purpose. Challenge yourself to create a legacy goal.

## Summary

Hopefully, the exercises you have been doing in this chapter will help you acquire some new insights about yourself. In this last chapter, we are expanding the metaphoric possibilities with particular emphasis on the journey, life as a book, and the legacy. A long list of other metaphoric options are also presented. By viewing your life/career through these different lenses, there is an opportunity to increase creativity and flexibility.

In coming to the end of the book, we trust that you have benefited from the career exploration exercises and the overall focus on the career flow metaphor. The book is designed with hope at the center and then movement through the various phases of career development—self-reflection, self-clarity, visioning, goal setting and planning, implementing, and adapting.

## Questions for Reflection and Discussion

1. What metaphor was Aaron initially using to define his career experience?

2. Have you had an experience where you changed your perspective on a situation by using a different metaphor? If so, describe what happened.

3. In this book, we describe the need for a different metaphor (career flow) to fit the current economic and social situation. What other metaphors might fit well with this change?

# Index

# Notes

**Notes**

**Notes**

# Notes

**Notes**

# Notes

# Notes

# Notes

# Notes